RUMINATIONS BY A DERVISH JAZZ PROFESSOR.

or

The Survival of an African Spirituality Amidst the Oral Traditions of the Trans-Atlantic Slavery Diaspora.

by

M.K.E.S.Lange. BA Hons. MA. PhD. Literary Theory & Cultural History. Dip H.E. Youth & Community. Cert. Client Centered Therapy-Carl Rogers Method. Cert TESOL.

Preface.

Section One: Orality.

An Oral Polemic.

Oral Poetry as Cultural Resistance.

An Oral Literate Continuum.

Section Two: Suggested Historical Archetypes of Contemporary Black Performance Poetry.

The First Poetic Archetype: The Griot of West Africa.

The Second Poetic Archetype: The Gospel Preacher.

The Third Poetic Archetype: The Blues Men & Women.

The Fourth Poeti Archetype: The Jazz Poets.

Section Three: Live and Direct.

Freedom Flavoured Fractals.

Self Defining Black Art

It's In The Mix.

"Consciousness is nothing but conscious social existence".

Karl Marx.

"The ability to define is the ability to control". Imamu Amiri Baraka/Leroi Jones.

"...so mongrel as I am, something prickles in me when I see the word Ashanti as with the word Warwickshire...both baptising their neither proud nor ashamed bastard, this hybrid..." Derek Walcott.

Preface.

My intention when I began this study was to write about my observations of Black performance poetry, and the meaning of the art form, in the context of Black U.K. today. This analysis would be developed in relation to how I had understood it as a participant observer of the past fifteen years, travelling the length and breadth of the country, and abroad working alongside, meeting, talking, and sharing ideas with many poets of all races. Part of this would be to explore the syncretic approach that blended music and poetry and various styles, as an aesthetic in itself. This aesthetic I discovered was associated with the oral nature of the poetry, and its ancestry in the oral tradition of the Griot of West Africa. To help me elaborate on this point I have drawn on the work of several people from a variety of related fields, the first is ethnomusicologist, and social theorist John Miller Chernoff. In his book African Rhythm and African Sensibility: Aesthetics and Social Action in Musical Idioms. Chernoff sheds light on the relationship between an African aesthetics based on orality, and the diasporan approach to creativity 1.

Professor of American studies, author, and recording artist Ben Sidran takes this idea a step further when he illustrates in his book Black Talk: How the Music of Black America Created a Radical Alternative to the Values of Western Literary Tradition, how 'Black music' whether it be Negro Spirituals, Gospel, Blues, R&B, Jazz, Funk, Reggae, Calypso, or Soul has always expressed, consciously or not, its African 'oral' heritage. He adds to this the notion that, part of this diasporan heritage has been, the use of this orality and music, to reflect the conditions of a minority Black culture in the midst of a white majority 2. It is with this notion in mind that I will be attempting to illustrate that there is a growing awareness amongst Black performance poets in the Britain, of the polemic inherent within this oral form of aesthetics, and that it can be seen to have survived in the varieties of music based oral poetry that can be found throughout the Black British communities of today. By way of illustration I will trace the emergence of a contemporary form from a long diasporic tradition, and analyse how at various points in history, poetry and music have been utilised as a means of expressing Black peoples lived experiences throughout the post-slavery, trans-Atlantic African diaspora, up until the present time.

These pan-diasporan cultural influences found amongst Black Britons, are what Jamaican Cultural theorist Stuart Hall refers to as, 'repertoires of Black popular culture' 3. He adds that these forms are impure, and to some degree hybridised from a vernacular base. They are already adaptations, moulded to the mixed, contradictory space of popular culture. Hall then describes how certain modes combined become signifiers of Blackness. It is this mixing that comes to signify the 'Black' in the notion of a 'Black community' as a repository of the oral techniques and forms that I will be exploring as I trace my aesthetic continuum of a diasporan oral tradition. This 'Black community', spoken of by Stuart Hall, is also 'the place where these traditions are kept, and whose struggles survive in persistence of the 'Black experience', that is the historical experience of Black people in the diaspora' (Hall S. 1995. p.28).

With reference to Hall's work I have attempted in the second part of my study to formulate a historical view of the sources of these 'cultural repertoires' in the form of 'poetic archetypes'. I have also attempted to isolate with the help of cultural historian Geneva Smitherman author of Black Talk: Words and Phrases from the Hood to the Amen Corner 4, and ethnomusicologist, and musician Alan Lomax, author of The Land Where The Blues Began, examples of what the components of these repertoires might be.

In the third part of my study I will be focusing on how these historical 'poetic archetypes', as embodiments of Hall's repertoires have provided cultural references points, in the form of the Griot of West Africa 5, the Gospel Preacher, and the Blues artist, and as a contemporary conjuncture of all three the Jazz poet. The aim will be to, illustrate how these focal points help facilitate the desire, on behalf of Black performance poets in the UK. to articulate their difference, in various ways. This articulation of difference being one of the ways that the poets, as Black people bearing the weight of the many negative representations of Black people that proliferate throughout Britain today 6, reinvent themselves through poetry, firstly as a means of resisting the hegemony of the white majority 7. This reconfiguration operates, secondly in relation to their diasporan relatives in the Americas and the Caribbean, and thirdly between the regional communities of Black Britain .

I will draw on the work of some of the UK.'s longest standing Black performance poets, and some of those more recently emerged, all of whom I have met, worked with, and or seen in performance, in order to illustrate how the oral nature of these cultural components allows for the construction of a performance poetry that is part of a specifically Black British lived experience. Although drawing on a variety of Black diasporan forms or strains of oral poetry, for example Jazz poetry and Dub-poetry. It is the way that these forms come together in the UK., in the work of specific artists, and the regional additions and linguistic fusions and nuances, that give the form a particularly UK. flavour. The history of a Black presence in

Britain, and the details of that existence and experience also serve to colour not only form but content and subject matter, and the struggle to define and control form.

Notes on Preface.

1 Chernoff's study has a lot in common with Sidran's in the way it relates diasporan musical forms to their African ancestry, an ancestry that is primarily rooted in orality. Both juxtapose the literate and the sedimentary approach to form, and the oral with the actional and extemporaneous approach to creativity. Both describe the relationship between the actionality of the oral culture, and an aesthetic based on social values that promotes the active involvement of the audience. Both emphasise the importance of music within Black communities as a vehicle for the addressing of social issues.

2 Another key text that deals with the way in which Black musical idioms reflect and comment on social conditions, is Frank Kofsky's Black Nationalism and the Revolution in Music, Pathfinder, 1970, New York. Kofsky's cultural and sociological study looks at the role of Jazz and the people who played it, in the context of the late fifties/early sixties, and the early rise in Black Nationalism amongst Jazz artists and listeners in post-World War Two America. There are some interesting interviews with Jazz giants John Coltrane and McCoy Tyner, and chapters on Amiri Baraka's Blues People. The final chapter deals with the role of Malcolm X and his attitude towards Black music, and the impact he had on Black musicians. Both the work of Malcolm X, and the movement in Black Jazz at this time being fundamental to the development of New York Jazz poetry collective The Last Poets. The Last Poets are the most singular influence on Black performance poetry in Britain, their early albums

have acquired the status of seminal texts amongst Black poets in general (see section three).

3 In his essay 'What is the 'Black' in Black Popular Culture' Stuart Hall describes the syncretic, hybrid nature of Black creativity thus:

'However deformed, incorporated, and inauthentic are the forms in which Black people and Black communities and traditions appear and are represented in popular culture, we continue to see, in the figures and the repertoires on which popular culture draws, the experiences that stand behind them. In its expressivity, its musicality, its orality, in its rich, deep, and varied attention to speech, in its inflections towards the vernacular and the local, in its rich production of counternarratives, and above all, in its metaphorical use of the musical vocabulary...' Hall S. 1992. Black Popular Culture p. 27. Ed. Gina Dent, Bay Press, Seattle.

4 Geneva Smitherman has some interesting things to say that link the oral tradition of Black America to the historical struggle for Black liberation, which she also charts with reference to key figures in that struggle. In her study Black Talk she asserts that, 'the Black Church has been the single most significant force in nurturing the surviving African language and cultural traditions of African-America'. She explains how the Church has been a rich reservoir of terms and expressions, and that it is responsible for keeping a large part of the oral tradition alive. She also outlines the influence of the Church on many of African-America's Black vocalists from James Brown and Aretha Franklin to today's Rap-poets. Smitherman's book also sheds some interesting light on Black oral practises like 'semantic inversion', the act of

taking words and turning them into their opposites. In her introduction she explains how African-Americans stake their claim on the English language, and at the same time reflect distinct Black values that are often at odds with European standards, the example she gives is the use of the word 'fat' to mean excellent or desirable, now spelt 'phat' in Black Hip-Hop circles, this term acknowledges the African notion that human body weight is aesthetically desirable, hence the African-American expression 'don't nobody want no bone' Geneva Smitherman, 1994, Black Talk p. 18, Houghton Mifflin, New York.

5 D.T. Niane's book Sundiata: An Epic of Old Mali, which is a written translation by G.D. Picket of the traditional history of the foundation of the medieval empire of Mali as handed down by oral tradition from generation to generation of 'Griots'. In his translation Picket offers a definition of the term 'Griot' thus:

I have not found the word 'Griot' in any dictionary, English or French, but it is used by Trimingham and is , in any case, better than the other words which approach but do not entirely express its meaning, e.g. minstrel, jester, herald, annalist, troubadour, poet. The Griot (pron. greeo) combined all these functions and the whole book is an illustration of what a Griot was.' (G.D. Picket. 1965. Longmans. London p. ix)

Picket refers to J.Spencer Trimingham, former Professor of History at The American University of Beirut, and author of Islam in West Africa 1959, Clarendon Press and A History of Islam in West Africa 1962, Oxford Uni.Press, in both books there is considerable attention paid to the role of, and the presence of Griots.

6   To illustrate the socio-cultural environment of Black people living in Britain today, in any great detail, is not the aim of this study. But in order to look at Black performance poetry in Britain I will be focusing on those poets who have been performing since the mid-seventies, and as such the following texts may help give some sort of background to the poetry, and the poets in terms of historical context. A more comprehensive account of the overall environment from which, Black British performance poetry has emerged is beyond the scope of this study. The following texts provide a useful canvass for viewing the outline I am about to sketch. The Black Press in Britain, I. Benjamin, 1995, Trentham Books, Stoke-on-Trent, describes how the emergence of the Black Press in Britain grew out of the demand for a representative voice, a voice that redresses the balance of a discriminatory mainstream media, another book that sets out to deal with the same issue is John Twitchin Ed. 1988, The Black and White Media Show: Hand Book for the Study of Racism and Television. Trentham books, London.

Dr. Aaron Haynes 1983 The State of Black Britain Roots Book, London.

1982 The Empire Strikes Back: Race & Racism in 70's Britain, Centre for Contemporary Cultural Studies, Uni.of Birmingham, Routledge London and New York.

Peter Fryer, 1984 Staying Power: The History of Black People in Britain .Pluto Press.

A. Sivanandan, 1982 A Different Hunger: Writings on Black Resistance. Pluto Press.

7 The 'winning of consent to unequal class relations' is my basic working definition of the term 'Hegemony', based on my interpretation of Gramsci's (1971) concept found

in Key Concepts In Communication, 1991, Routledge, p.102. For example Black people who happily sing songs like 'The Ghetto is Our Home', in a way that not only legitimates their social position, but seems to almost celebrate their own oppression, are suffering under hegemony. Hegemony being 'the ability in certain historical periods of the dominant classes to exercise social and cultural leadership, and by means-rather than by direct coercion of subordinate classes to maintain their power over the economic, cultural and political direction of the nation' (ibid). As in the notion of a cosy ghetto home, that makes sense of the world in a way that fits in with the interests of the hegemonic alliance of classes, or power bloc. The acceptance by Black people of a notion of race based on skin colour, it could be argued, is itself a form of hegemony.

Section One: Orality.

An Oral Polemics.

I have mentioned a polemics associated with a Black diasporan 1 tradition of orature, a form of social critique born from the experience of life as a marginalised racial group in British society. I have suggested that despite displacement, relocation, or dissemination through various networks of communication and cultural exchange over the passage of time, artistic products and aesthetic codes may be traceable back to experiences that form a specific type of response. A response that although it may appear differently in terms of its stylistic expression for example Jazz-poetry and Dub-poetry have distinctly different sounds, in terms of practice there are similarities in the way their content reflects the life experiences of the poet. The poets respond to life in their communities, whether in Kingston, Brixton, or the Bronx by writing about it, their work when compared side by side relates a common experience and a common response throughout the diaspora 2. A common response to a common experience of racial subjugation. The response relies upon the proposition that some cultural, religious, and linguistic affiliations can be identified, as Paul Gilroy suggests (Gilroy P. 1993 p. 81).

African-American literary critic Henry L. Gates Jr. believes that race is a metaphor for something else, and not an end in itself, apart from its creation by an act of language (Gates H.L.1986. p. 15). He describes how Black readers of literature in English, are 'confronted by a collective and racist text of themselves which Europeans have invented' (Gates ibid). What Gates is talking about here is like Edward Said's notion of 'Orientalism' 3, a situation where in, even the most well meaning representations of Black life, in much of what has been canonised as 'English Literature' traditionally, are still merely representations of a Black 'other', and do not speak from a lived experience. Joseph Conrad's book about colonialism in the Belgian Congo, Heart of Darkness is a prime example of how a sympathetic, in theory anti-colonialist text, due to the historic and cultural location of its author, and the limits of his experience, is still the purveyor of an implicit notion of white supremacy 4.

Benjamin Zephania, Levi Tafari, Linton Kwesi Johnson, SuAndi, Muhammad Yusef and Lemn Seisay, are just a few examples of Black British performance poets who see the conscious decision to align themselves and their art form with an oral tradition as a political act 5.

The people I have mentioned see their work as poets as part of the struggle to define their art forms according to an aesthetic that in some way supports the autonomy of the Black artist. The oral nature of Black performance poetry creates a space from which the artist can operate free from the restrictions of the written language, simply because of the role 'sound' plays in identifying the speaker, a point I will also elaborate on later. Many of the British Black performance poets that I have spoken with, agree that oral poetry offers the opportunity to construct, and continually reinvent a Black British identity that is part of a 'lived and evolving experience'. This experience uses the cultural practise of oral poetry, as part of, and the overall eclecticism of diasporan repertoires, as a form of cultural resistance, where in traditional musical forms and working methods pass on social values. The improvisational, flexible nature of orality as a form allows for the adherence to communitarianism, without denying the individual artist their individual expression of that group experience 6. The immediate call and response feedback, being a regulatory form of criticism, that operates on the artist performing in a live context.

I will explore, in social terms, the need for the poetry to be performed orally, in relation to its various functions historically. This in turn will inform us to how, the peculiarities of form that are distinctive of, if not unique to, Black performance poetry in Britain, are tied into the common lived experience of Black people across the diaspora, as a racially subjugated people. To conduct this exploration I will be comparing the two main overall distinguishing characteristics of Black performance poetry, its orality, and its musicality, and how these elements aid the Black performance poet by facilitating the continual reinvention of the Black self in terms acceptable to that self. If our identities are the names we give to the different ways we are positioned by, and position ourselves in narratives of the past, then my purpose will be an imaginative reconstruction of a usable past, to engage the 'socio-cultural' in what Edmund Burke might call 'a partnership of past and present' (Gates H.L. Dent G. ed. 1992. 76-77). This will take the form of an analysis of diasporan oral forms, that relates to the survival of a set of Spiritual and moral based values, historically encapsulated within, and uniting the changing styles and forms of Black oral performance, be it Gospel Preaching, Talking Blues, Dub Ranting, or Jazz Oration, oral forms and communitarian values that both inform and unite, the art of Black orature throughout the diaspora, up to today and the performance poetry of Britain's Black urban communities.

Notes on An Oral Polemics.

1 A note on racial terminology: Although the concept of race has no scientific validity, it functions as an ideological weapon to achieve political ends, the most basic being slavery, but also including policies of apartheid, immigration, and employment. As such 'racism' a discourse that allows the simple delineation of racial categories along the lines of such things as skin colour exists (From an unpublished paper by Ross Dawson, 'Imperialism and colonialism: intersections' 1996). As Franz Fanon states: ' Wherever he goes the Negro remains a Negro' (Black Skins, White Masks, p.173).

Stuart Hall has described 'Black' as:

'...an extraordinary diversity of subjective positions, social experiences and cultural identities which compose the category 'black'; that is, the recognition that 'black' is essentially a politically and culturally constructed category, which cannot be grounded in a set of fixed transcultural or transcendental racial categories and which therefore has no guarantees in nature', 1989, 'New Ethnicities', Black Film, British Cinema ICA Document 7, Institute of Contemporary Arts. See also 'Race and Racism: A Symposium' 1995, with an introduction by Tricia Rose and Andrew Ross, from Social Text 42, and Multiculturalism: A Critical Reader 1994, Ed. D. Theo Goldberg, Blackwell, also 'Racism and Culture' Kadiatuh Kanneh, 1993, Paragraph: A Journal of Modern Critical Theory, Vol. 16, No. 1, March. Edinburgh Uni. Press, and Frantz Fanon 1967 The Wretched of The Earth, Penguin, with an introduction by Homi Bhabha, and Homi Bhabha's Nation and Narration 1990 Routledge, and The Location of Culture, Bhabha H., 1994.

2 Diaspora: A new ethic of cultural diversity, opposing an old appeal to essence and purity, is occasioned by the widespread experience of diaspora, the dispersion of ethnic communities. There is a celebration of heterogeneity and cultural plurality. This can be aligned with such terms as hybridity, syncretism, and creolization (From an unpublished paper by Ross Dawson, 'Imperialism and colonialism: intersections' 1996).

3 Edward Said, 1978, 'Latent and Manifest Orientalism' Orientalism, Routledge, p. 329-343.

4 See The section on Chinua Achebe in Heart of Darkness: A Critical Collection Ed. R. Kinborough, A Norton Critical Collection, 1988. Achebe comments disfavourably on Conrad's portrayal of the 'native' 6, and his omission of any

positive images that actually put the African on an equal basis as human beings. When the 'cannibal' is taught to stoke the boiler, it is described as miraculous as, 'seeing a dog standing up on its hind legs wearing breeches and smoking a pipe'.

5 As performance poets, both SuAndi and Merle Collins are working as cultural historians following a line of thought that goes beyond 'either-or-isms' of a Black or British binary, they have moved into a 'both-and' form of awareness that is not unlike Gilroy's notion of a 'conceptual logic of supplementarity' (Gilroy. 1995. p. 68). This comes from the desire to make art of being both Black and British. This is something that Gilroy states should be part of the micro-political task of recoding the cultural core of national life, in order to eventually leave ethnic absolutism behind.

6 See 'Jazz Text'': Voice and Improvisation in Poetry, Jazz and Song", 1991 Journal of Popular Music, Vol. 13, No.12p. 151, Hartman &Co. Princeton.

Oral Poetry as Cultural Resistance.

Oral tradition as a form of social comment can be seen from the earliest days on the plantation, and the stories of 'Old John' an early plantation incarnation of the Trickster, Esu Elegba of the Yoruba narrative tradition, through to the emergence of Frederick Douglas and the first slave narrative, up until more recent times with the advent of the civil rights movement, and the struggle against apartheid, there has been a strong oral tradition amongst people of African descent that has commented on the social conditions of the time, sometimes in a humorous, satirical way, sometimes in a mournful melancholy manner, sometimes in a venting of pure rage. This orality is what shapes the poetry.

'Black performance poetry' is the poetry being performed in clubs, bars, cafes, arts centres, theatres, at meetings, rallies, funerals and weddings by Black people. This is a poetry whose form, and content, are both evolving from, and influenced by, the variety of converging musical forms, and modes of verbal interaction that have emerged from the lived experience of Black people within the diaspora 1. For The Griot Workshop Black poetry has become synonymous with the collective ritual of performance 2. One of the major objectives of the thesis will be to examine those characteristics that make Black performance poetry in Britain, a ritualistic group experience. This will involve mainly distinguishing what the priorities of the oral practitioner are as somebody who is immediately in contact with their audience, as opposed to the poet whose contact with their audience is via the word on the page. Caribbean poet, literary critic, and historian Edward Kamau Brathwaite emphasises this division when he describes reading as an isolated, individualistic expression. The oral tradition, which he relates to the Griot, demands the audience to complete the community 'the noise and sounds that the maker makes are responded to by the audience and are returned to him. Hence we have the creation of a continuum where meaning truly resides' (Brathwaite E.K. 1984. p. 17-18). Brathwaite also describes how, what he calls, 'total expression' comes about, 'because people live in conditions of poverty, because they come from a historical experience where they had to rely on their very breath rather than paraphernalia like books and museums and machines. They had to depend on immanence, the power within themselves, rather than the technology outside themselves' (ibid). Ben Sidran's study echoes Brathwaite's ideas from an African-American angle 3. It is for this reason that the Black British poets that I have mentioned, see the role of the Black performance poet, as custodian of a collective heritage. In St Vincent, and Belize the Garifuna people use the term 'Keepers of the Flame'. Like Brathwaite's Griot, people like Zephania, Tafari, Suandi and Yusef are self proclaimed defenders of the communitarian values rooted in a sense of social responsibility, cultural awareness, and a shared history of racial subjugation. This experience of racial subjugation is a lived experience, an experience common to many Black people throughout the African diaspora. I will explore how these values, contained in the archetype of 'The Griot', have been nurtured and preserved in such institutions as Negro Spirituals sung by the slaves on the plantations, the Gospel Churches, in the art of the archetypal Black Preacher, and the Blues artist. I will illustrate how there is still a resonance of these key archetypal figures, in the form of poetic expression that comes together as Black performance poetry in Britain today. The archetypal Griot and the original African music based culture 4 supplies the oral components for the poetic form, as used today in Britain by the Black performance poet. Many of these components, which I will elaborate on in more detail later, have origins that are related to the forms of cultural expression practised in institutions like the Gospel Churches, the Blues-dance, and the Jam-session.

Poets like, SuAndi, Levi Tafari, and Muhammad Yusef et al, deal with the traditional relationship between music and poetry in the Black community as a way of identifying with the group 5. The fact that this is a tradition of music and poetry that is seldom recognised, and has largely been the victim of the selective tradition of Western literary disciplines that have placed an emphasis on the written word over the spoken word, is often used by poets to emphasise the 'Blackness' of the form, by emphasising its 'otherness'. Another aspect of orality that is used to identify the 'Blackness' of the poetic form is the variety of ways that Black people speak English throughout the diaspora. Edward Kamau Brathwaite elaborates on this point when he describes how: 'It may be in English but often it is in an English which is like a howl, or a shout or a machine gun or the wind or a wave (ibid p. 13)'. As such if there is a form of empowerment within the performing of poetry orally, for Black people it is an empowerment that resides in the difference between an oral poetry and a written form of poetry. A difference that allows the poet the freedom to diverge from Western tradition in order to reinvent himself free from the prejudices of White supremacy, while still using the language of that society. The problem of trying to articulate a Black experience in English is exemplified in the words of Mikhail Bakhtin when he states;

'...language, for the individual consciousness, lies on the borderline between oneself and the other. The word in language is half someone else's. It becomes "one's own" only when the speaker postulates it with his (or her) own intention, his (or her) own accent, when he (or she) appropriates the word, adapting it to his (or her) own semantic and expressive intention. Prior to this...it exists in peoples mouths, other people's contexts, serving other people's intentions',
(Mikhail Bakhtin. 1976. p. 176-196).

When Black people speak the English language, like working class people who may have regional inflections in their mode of speech, they immediately put a stamp on the words they use, a stamp that identifies their difference by the sound they make. This appropriation is achieved as much with sound as it is with vernacular disruptions of grammar or colloquial twists in syntax. As Caribbean poet and theorist Edward Kamau Braithwaite explains the poetry of the oral tradition, like the language of his particular part of the African diaspora, exists not in a dictionary but in the tradition of the spoken word 6 . He describes how it is based as much on sound as it is on song, the noise that it makes being part of the meaning, he adds that when it is written you loose the sound, and as such part of the meaning. The adding of this identity-specific sound is what stops the word being someone else's, and makes it ones own 7. In relation to Bakhtin's quote, it is because of the ability to stake a claim on the language more easily with the voice than the pen that the oral poet can more easily avoid what Bakhtin describes as 'serving other peoples intentions'. One example of this is how the word 'bad' can mean 'good' in Black vernacular expression, an expression that although it may have started in African-American circles has spread across the diaspora and beyond, to the extent that it has taken on a literate form and acquired a spelling of its own as in the often seen 'badd'. Everyone knows that when Michael Jackson sings ' I'm Badd ', he actually means 'I'm great'. Actually from a Mandingo expression to be badly good, so good it was bad.

It is in this way that oral poetry is positioned in tension with, or against, and with the awareness of the imperialistic legacy of such concepts as Matthew Arnold's notion of 'high culture'. A notion that prescribed and established, for the masses, what they should consider to be 'the best that has been thought and said in the world' 8. Notions like 'great literature', 'fine' art, and 'serious' music are associated with the values of an imperial colonialist past. In the eyes of Black oral poets like SuAndi, Yusef, et al, such forms are seen to represent, a form of cultural imperialism. This is one of the reasons why, as Brathwaite stipulates Black oral poetry largely ignores pentameter 9 as part of the process of the decolonization of the process of cultural production, and the very word 'culture' itself 10. This fact alone sets the Black performance poet apart from the more academically influenced exponent of Black poetry who may have learned his or her craft within the academies of the Western literary tradition, a craft that may rely more on the written word as their source of inspiration, and generic heritage, as well as European literary figures, models, and forms. The commitment of the oral poet to the communal values of the spoken form are a conscious act of resistance like the struggle to dismantle the supremacy of elite, high English culture and its colonisation of the working classes as championed by Richard Hoggart in 1957, and Raymond Williams in 1958 11.

As an awareness of the importance of documenting the Black experience in an autonomous manner became more of an issue amongst Black artists and poets, so did the idea that 'recieved English' was too restrictive for the expression of a Black experience. As this notion spread the more critical exponents of the oral forms laid an emphasis on dialect, feel, attitude, regional accent, and musicality in order to capture the specifics of the Black ethos that they knew existed within their cultural sphere of poetic activity. African-American poet and cultural activist, Amiri Baraka, and Afro-Caribbean poet and literary critic, Edward Kamau Brathwaite, both academics known for performing their work in public, contributed to this movement. Brathwaite championed what he called 'nation language', which was his term for Caribbean patois, or Creole. He argued that the term dialect carried pejorative connotations, and that dialect was thought of as bad English, or inferior English (Brathwaite E.K. 1984.p. 17). He argued that dialect was something you used to make fun of someone, and that 'Caricature speaks in dialect', in much the same way that white comedian Jim Davidson does, with his, 'West Indian' character 'Chalky', who is very unpopular amongst Black people 12. For Brathwaite Nation language was the submerged area of that dialect, he adds:

'It may be in English...It is also like the Blues. And sometimes it is English and African at the same time' (Ibid.p.13).

From his position within the diaspora, Amiri Baraka's analysis why the poetry should be oral echoed Brathwaite's in many ways as he proselytised about what Brathwaite had called the previously reviled, but now revitalised, 'inner movement in language - its orality'. Baraka talked about a Blues sensibility being codified into an aesthetic that 'shows out in everything done, not just the music' (Salaam.K.Y.1994. p.10). He characterized a 'new Black poetry', in relation to this aesthetics, a poetry that was 'mostly to do with rhythm, images, and sound'. To link Baraka's work back to Brathwaite and Bakhtin's statements about how a poet sounds, I would like to quote Dent and Bryan's break-down of Baraka's Blues aesthetic as they observed it in practice:

'In terms of rhythm, the poetry had to dance, to

ride/be/hear/feel: the images can/should connect one consciousness with another's, and would often come from Blues (Blues singers where our first heavy poets' (Dent T. & Bryan V.H. 1993. p. 134).

This shift in emphasis led to a further development in the liberation of an existent, yet historically, suppressed Black voice amongst Black poets in Britain. Black appropriation of English, as the language of the dominant elite, yet a language that held meaning for Black people in the UK., historically can be seen the way Black performance poet Mikey Smith, in a televised discussion with C.L.R.James, changed the name Shakespeare to Shaka's Spear. All of a sudden an icon of Anglified authenticity became a symbol of Black resistance, and without losing its original meaning, or usage as a symbolically English icon in the form of a person's name, it became the name linked to an African symbol of Black Resistance.

It is interesting to note that when Britain colonised Kenya it introduced the notion of 'the Queen's Swahili' into the culture, this was a standardised form used mainly by civil servants. After independence people who spoke only 'Queens Swahili', and could not talk in a colloquial form were often stigmatised as lackeys of the oppressive colonial forces. Many Black intellectuals throughout the United States and the Caribbean took directives from the various struggles for independence throughout the colonised main land of Africa, even upuntill the eighties Ngugi wa'Thiongo was championing the cause of a decolonizing of the tongue in an effort to decolonize the mind. Performance poet John Agard describes a diasporan attempt at linguistic subversion in his poem 'Listen Mr. Oxford don':

I'm not a violent man Mr. Oxford don

I only armed wit mih human breath
but human breath is a dangerous weapon
So mek dem send one big word after me
I ent serving no jail sentence
I slashing suffix in self defence
I bashing future wit present tense
and if necessary
I making de Queen's English accessory
to my offence. (Agard J. 1985. p.44).

Although a common root in the language and history of England remains one of the main things that Black British performance poetry has in common with its diasporan relatives, an African heritage that blurs the boundaries between poetry, music, dance, spirituality, religion and visual art is the other. Black performance poetry in Britain, like its African progenitor is a cultural space where social issues, poetry and music all have difficulty existing without each other.

Notes on Oral Poetry as Cultural Resistance.

1 This is what Stuart Hall calls 'the repertoire of Black popular culture' i.e. style, a deep attachment to music, and the use of the body (Hall S. Dent G.Ed. 1992.p. 28).

2 In the introduction to SuAndi's book of poetry Style in Performance, Merle Collins in describing the work of 'sister poet' SuAndi, had this to say:

'The life of Black Britain includes a range of experiences and this is one of many voices, with its particular aspects of body language, all of which contributes to the overall beauty of the work. SuAndi plays various roles, presents various experiences and the voice of actress/story teller is always there. SuAndi is part of a tradition of Black poets in Britain who give spoken presentations (or performances) of their work. The work is often referred to as performance poetry, perhaps because it is restoring Black poetry to its roots of dialogue, commentary and intimate recordings of a people's story, it presents a reality that is difficult to analyse within a tradition which has come to depend exclusively on a disembodied written word which sometimes seeks to divorce itself from reality. But SuAndi's achievement here proves that she is part of a tradition that is both oral and written.

It is part of the work of griots who have for centuries recorded the history of African people in poetry, in song, in chant, in story. It is part of an entire generation, part of the story of a race, is part of the story of a woman of a face'

(SuAndi. 1990. p.4. Intro. by Merle Collins.)

3 See Ben Sidran, 1971, Chapter 1 'Oral Culture and Musical Tradition: Prehistory and early History (theory), Black talk: How The Music of Black America Created a Radical Alternative to the Values of Western Literary Tradition, with a forward by Jazz saxophonist and poet Archie Schepp.

4 Kamau Brathwaite states 'music is the surest threshold to the language that comes out of it', he links the oral tradition to ritualistic forms of worship like 'Shango' and 'Kumina', which also have as in the African tradition their own specific forms of music and drum accompaniment, The History of the Voice. New Beacon Book. 1984, p. 18. Brathwaite also notes a variety of essays that outline the relationship between such forms as Calypso and poetry, Blues and poetry, Kaiso and poetry, Reggae and poetry, and Jazz and poetry, p. 16-19.

5 Liverpool Dub-poet Levi Tafari describes his poetry as having an 'in built Reggae rhythm', From an interview at the poets home June 7th, 1996.

6 See Levi Tafari's 'Duboetry':

'Duboetry's not in your dictionary
No its inna different category
So learn to chant Duboetry
Make it part of your vocabulary' (1989. Liverpool Experience).

7 See Monroe K. Spears Essay on 'Black English', and his reference to 'stage darkies'. Also his note on 'bidialecticism', Talking' and Testifyin': The Language of Black America, Houghton Mifflin 1977, Ed Geneva Smitherman .p.169.

8 See Key Concepts in Communication 1991, Eds.Tim O'Sullivan, John Hartley, Danny Saunders, John Fiske, p. 59, there is an interesting note on 'culture' as an embattled perfection offering an ideology to goverment elites, administrative, intellectual and even broadcasting circles within which their sectional interests can be represented as general interests.

9 Brathwaite describes what he calls the 'bass-based reggae-canter of downbeat on the first syllable of the first and second bars, followed by a syncopation on the third, followed by full offbeat/downbeats on the fourth', as one of the music inspired forms replacing the pentameter, ibid p. 24.

10 'Culture is now seen as a determining and not just a determined part of social activity, and therefore culture is

a significant sphere for the reproduction of social power inequalities' see Key Concepts in Communication, 1991.

11 The work of Hoggart and Williams, as an initiative has now been taken up by 'cultural studies', in which the concept of culture has undergone a move towards being defined as 'The institutionally or informally organised social production and reproduction of sense, meaning and consciousness', ibid p. 59.

12 See Tommy L. Lott 'Black Vernacular Representation and Cultural Malpractice', Multiculturalism: A Critical Reader, Ed. David Theo Goldberg, Blackwell, 1994.

An Oral Literate Continuum.

There are some key differences between the oral culture of today's Black performance poet and that of his archetypal ancestor the Griot, but they are not as fundamental as we might at first imagine. Orality and literacy are not two separate and independent things, they do mutually interact 1. The form of oral culture that I will be referring to in this debate are classified by Ong as 'secondary' forms of oral culture. Orality and literacy are not two separate and independent worlds as we have noted, and as such a secondary oral culture is one born of this interaction 2. As Gates has suggested Black oral literary forms can merge with received (European) literary forms to create new (and distinctly Black) genres of literature (Gates. 1984). The Blackness is the hybridity, not only in terms of the cross pollination of diasporan forms as mentioned previously, but also the syncretic appropriation of European cultural aesthetics. If the development of the written word is Europe's contribution to Black poetry then Africa's contribution rests in its fusing of the genres of music, poetry, dance and theatre.

In respect of this interdisciplinary approach to Black performance poetry, there can be seen an actionality, by this I mean an important use of the body as a medium for poetic communication. Ntozake Shange has described this actionality like this: 'Part of how we speak is musical. We are not alienated from our bodies, not resistant to respond to music, not inhibited by loud saxophones, our culture is visual, oral...movement, music, dance, have all got to be worked into the syntax of our language' (Owusu K. 1985. .p.134). Already we can see how Black poetic expression, in its oral form opens up levels of communication that include the non-verbal.

'Orature' as it is described by Cecil Gutzmore: 'is an emerging politicised radical African aesthetics. The concept of orature brings together a number of forms of performance in the arts which European aesthetics treats as distinct' (Ed. Kwesi Owusu,1988. ibid.p.279). What Gutzmore is talking about when he speaks of an emerging politicised aesthetics, is the awareness amongst Black performance poets of the social nature of their poetry, the very word 'performance' implies not just an audience, but an immediacy connected to some sort of collective gathering. The ritualistic role of the performance poet as a member of a collective, dealing with socially aware subject matter, whether performing within his own social group or to outsiders, echoes the conscience pricking practises of not just the Black Gospel preachers, but the pre-slavery, African village orators the Griots.

Notes on An Oral Literate Continuum.

1   Even before the slaves had contact with a literate European culture they had already been held under the influence of the Islamic literary world to some extent. African Griots from an oral culture like the Mandingo, or the Mende, with a predominantly illiterate population, would have interacted to large extant with the literate culture of Islam, especially in Sene-Gambia region, and throughout Mali. Many wrote in their own languages using Arabic script, read and wrote in the Arabic language also. At its high point as a centre of trade within the Islamic world, Timbuctoo sold more hand written books than any other commodity.

2 See Stuart Hall's, 1989, New Ethnicities Black Film, British Cinema ICA Documents 7, London Institute of Contemporary Arts. Also in Bill Ashcroft et al (eds) 1995, The Post Colonial Studies Reader, Routledge.

SectionTwo: Suggested Historical Arche-types of Contemporary Black Performance Poets.

The Griot of West Africa.

In the expressive culture of the African diaspora, a discursive economy emerges that encodes the refusal to subordinate the particularity of the slave experience, to the totalising power of 'universal reason' held exclusively in the hands of the dominant elite. The vernacular components of Black expressive culture, as seen in the performance poetry of the Black community in contemporary Britain, have survived in and are emerging from, the reproduction of a distinct political perspective in which, as Gilroy suggests 'autopoesis articulates with poetics to form a stance, a style, and a philosophical mood that have been repeated and reworked', in the political culture of the diaspora ever since (Gilroy P. 1993. p. 69-70).

It is my supposition that this continual reworking has been possible due to the irrepressible resonance of various key archetypal models, that reside in the historio-cultural past of the Black diaspora. Archetypal models encoded, the vernacular components of expressive culture, as employed by today's Black performance poet. I will be looking at how the influences of these archetypes are mediated in specific-historical situations, how they come together in the form and content of a specific type of performance poet today.

To aid me in my discussion I have isolated, what I consider to be, three of these archetypes. The first is a pre-slavery archetype, in the form of the Griot, the singer/historian, praise-poet/musician of West Africa, who is most often cited in Afrocentric constructions of an imaginary African past as the progenitor of today's oral poets, singers, and story tellers, from Rap artists, to Dub poets, Jazz poets and beyond.

The second is an arche-type that evolved from the actual experience of slavery itself, and the coming together of the traditions of the European Christian Church, and the remnants of an African form of worship, such as Voun Doun, or Ju-Ju, and that archetype is the Black preacher of Gospel Churches of the Southern States of America. There is a third archetypal figure in the Bluesman, often compared to the Griot in the way he recombined the sacred and the profane in a way that was closer to the African norm. Having said that there is a degree of over lap in all the arch typical models that I have suggested.

These overlaps are also reflected in the many varieties of exponents of the Black oral traditions throughout the diaspora and in Africa. It is in this area of confluence that the contemporary performance poet operates. It is in the resonance's of these archetypes that Black performance poetry in Britain aquires a meaning.

Sociologist John Miller Chernoff, on the role of music in African society, had this to say: 'music helps people to work, to enjoy themselves, to control a bad person or praise a good one, to recite history, poetry, and proverbs to celebrate a funeral, or a festival' (Chernoff, J.1979. p.167). The person who would have employed this music to praise, recite history, poetry and proverbs, or even to satirise an opponent, would have been the Griot. Griots have been the bards, the troubadours of West Africa from ancient times till today: 'they are musician, storyteller, singer, poet, and historian all in one person, they are Africa's counterpart to the medieval minstrel' (Habekost.1986. p.10).

Many of these Griots were also the repository of folk-lore and religious knowledge. Islam was carried from Arabia via the Sudan by Sufi counterparts to the Griot, their teachings were a form of mysticism, that involved drumming, dancing, chanting, and the reciting of poetry, often extemporaneously composed on the spot. One of the most well known forms of Sufi music in the Western world, and one that is compared to Jazz is the music of the Gnaoua 1.

The Griot as a lone troubadour has many names depending on region of origin, throughout Mali and the Sene-Gambia region they are known as Djele, Jelofo, Jali, Halam-khat, Gavel, Jare, and they exist from Sudan to Mali to Morocco as Gnaoua 2. The string accompanied tradition of oral poetry found amongst many of West Africa's

Griots belongs to the, Islamic inspired, thousand year old music tradition of Ancient Mali, and its accompanying oral literature which spreads throughout the Sene-Gambia region into Ghana and Northern Nigeria via the Mandingo, Hausa, Fulani, and the Senehure peoples 3.

The improvisational nature of the Griot's approach, and the creative pioneering approach to both music and language that allowed him to extemporaneously compose poetry on the spot, are what the African diasporan has retained of this ancient folk heritage. Another aspect of this folk art that has survived in the oral poetics of the diaspora is the infusion of these art forms with philosophy, and certain aspects of African religious ritual, for example the Sufi poet Abu-Said, son of Abi-Khair states: 'To be a Sufi is to detach from fixed ideas and from preconceptions'(Shah I.1968. Epigram). The philosophy behind this statement hints at the flexibility needed to be a good improviser 4.

It is interesting to note that the Koran, the holy scripture of Islam, was recited from the mouth of the prophet Muhammad (SAWS) in rhymed verses, as he was not able to write, and the whole Koran rhymes from beginning to end. The first followers of Islam learned these rhymes by heart as each was revealed, day by day over a period of twenty three years, as they chanted them daily as prayers, and as meditative techniques of focusing called 'dhikr', similar to the Hindu mantra 5. Even today the oral aspect is very important, there is meant to be at least one person in each community who can recite the whole book of the Koran from memory, this person is called The Hafiz. This tradition was maintained so that the words of the Koran could not be altered. The name 'Al Koran' means 'The Recital'. And the reciting of its words with 'tartil', which means 'spiritual adornment' and emotional precision, 'Soul Power' by any other name, is considered an art form 6. This tradition of memorising large pieces of oral literature, was not unusual amongst either the Arabs or the Africans. And in this way, even amongst the animist religions of Africa, oral literature prior to slavery played a big part in the passing on of ideas and cultural beliefs 7.

In the New World, because there was no split between the secular and the spiritual in African religious life, when the African took on Christianity 'his world extended spatially upward' (Levine 1971). Being continually in the presence of his God allowed the African-American, as he was becoming, to hold on to the certainty that within one's own lifetime' rebirth was continually possible' (Levine.L.W. 1971. p.114-126). The slaves held regular sessions of spiritual rebirth and conversion, and in these sessions they employed the earth-bow, a hole in the ground that acted as a resonator, with a piece of string held over it that was plucked like an acoustic bass, or a tea-chest bass of the sort used in skiffle bands. This accompanied 'testifying', and storytelling (Rawich.G.P. 1972. p.36-47).

The resonances of the Griot within the polyphonic, polymetrical, interrelated, intertwining nature of Black cultural components, are characteristics that where necessary to meet the demands of their active ritualistic, and ceremonial social practises during slavery. These poetic and musical activities were techniques of cognition linked to the overall philosophy and structure of African processes of socialisation. Music is essential to life in Africa because Africans use music to mediate their involvement within a community, a good musical performance reveals their orientation towards this concern. As John Miller-Chernoff states as a cultural expression, music is a product of this sense of social responsibility, the development of a musical awareness in Africa constitutes a process of education, 'music's explicit purpose, in the various ways it might be defined by Africans, is , essentially, socialisation' (Chernoff J.M. 1979. p. 154). Through music 'an individual learns the potentials and limitations of participation in a communal context dramatically arranged for the engagement, display, and critical examination of fundamental cultural values'(ibid), which form part of an elaborate set of generative themes patterning the experience of everyday life. In the midst of change they characterise a cultures continuity as they meet the realities of new situations. For the Black performance poet in today's Britain, an awareness of the cultural significance of music in the everyday lives of Black people, and an awareness of the cultural practise of orality, within an historical context, have become part of a diasporan set of generative themes.

As Linton Kwesi Johnson testifies in his poem 'Bass Culture', the bass sound, as described in the spiritual ritual of rebirth, has a key role in the Black ritual experience 8. In Bahia in North East Brazil, where the population is predominantly Black African, they have their own particular type of Samba sound called rolling thunder, which favours a deep bass sound through the extra use or surdus, bass-drums. The lower register producing a more physical sound, a sound more conducive to dancing, movement being a key prerequisite to many African rituals. A good deep drum and bass sound is said 'to make you wind up your waist and shake the body line' as a form of catharsis. The first Black dance music to evolve from a Black British situation that is neither derivative of the Caribbean or America, is Jungle, this music is also known by the name 'Drum and Bass'. Chernoff explains the relationship between rhythm, participation and power in the complex use of rhythm in African culture:

'The contrasting, tightly organised rhythms are powerful...because there is a vitality in rhythmic conflict, powerful precisely because people are affected and moved. As people participate in a musical situation, they mediate the conflict, and their immediate presence gives power a personal form so that they can relate to it' (Chernoff J.M. 1979.p.169).

It is not surprising that today's Black performance poetry, by often being accompanied by a beat, adds an aspect of physical participation to the communication process, when we understand that some of its origins lay in the oral traditions of the Griot and a culture where narrators rely on rhythmic communication as a means of making their words, and their message more attractive. It is this beat that acts as the spoon full sugar to the often unpleasant, and sometimes bitter medicine that the words of a poem may represent. It is the beat that invokes movement from the audience. I have witnessed performances where the audience have danced to the rhythm of the verbal delivery, before the music has even started this is not unusual. This aspect of rhythmic delivery when faced with a potentially tense crowd, can have a cathartic effect on that whole body of people. The rhythm causes a movement that comforts, and placates in the same way that the rocking motion of a Muslim or Jew during prayer does. This is what is meant by the use of rhythm as a means of group catharsis. This cathartic movement is linked to the rhythm in much the same way that the collective swing of the chain gang is, or the sound

of the work song as the slave 'totes that barge and lifts that bail', rhythmic acts not unrelated to the African womens' mortars hitting their pestles in time, until the whole process of work, or even suffering becomes sublimated within an act of musical involvement. Alan Lomax describes this social catharsis in action in a prayer meeting in the Mississippi Delta:
'Women were going into trance all over the little church. Talking in tongues: Haw-haw-haw-haw-haw,
Ta-tel iddle-iddle uh,
Ta-tel iddel-iddle uh.
Rolling on the floor. Acting out their tensions' (Lomax A. 1993. p. 103).

Linking this cathartic mode of worship to the specifics of the situation, Lomax believes along with others, that the high frequency of feminine possession in African ritual is due to a social overload. This is how he accounts for the similarity in response amongst some Gospel congregations, and Moroccan women engaging in an informal Zar ceremony. He explains how the women do more than half the agricultural work, and often are in charge of marketing activities in Africa. African-American women have not only borne a similar burden of work and responsibility, they have also suffered twin torments of poverty and low-class status, after slavery. Of course the twin torments of poverty and low-class status are things that were and still are experienced by Black men aswell as Black women today.

As an insight into the diasporan use of music as a means of socialisation, there are parallels to Miller-Chernoff's description of the members of an African drum ensemble and how they use music and rhythmic complexity to instigate social awareness 9. There is a similarity in how Ben Sidran describes a soloist in a Jazz combo 10 as both playing within and without the group, virtuosity depending on interaction with the group as an individual, while responding to the demands of the artistic moment in an individual manner, being part of what gets group approval. The 'Jam' session11 is in fact a ritual of integration, where people experiment in creating something new with known phrases and within a known rhythmic structure. This has to be accomplished in a way that reinforces the groups collective identity, while allowing the soloist to assert their own presence impressively. Like the drum soloist in Chernoff's African ensemble improvising with polyrhythmic phraseology, or the Jazz soloist in a combo improvising with rhythmic phrasing to fit the overall groove, the oral poet working with drums, often mediates the rhythmic phrasing of his words to create a polyrhythmic effect that is often pleasing, or recognisably familiar, to the listener. This going with the established flow is called riding the rhythm, while at the same time a Black performance poet is often described by, and commended on the way he 'drops lyrics', this being a comment on his particular flair for unique delivery 12. Within the act of performance poetry we can see a modern parallel to the mediation between poet and audience. As Ralph Ellison has stated in his essay 'Blues People' first published in Shadow Act, The New York Review of Books, Feb. 6th, 1964, p. 249-250,:

' True Jazz is an art of individual assertion within and against the group. Each true jazz moment springs from a contest in which the artist challenges all the rest, each solo flight, or improvisation, represents a definition of his identity as an individual, and as a member of the collectivity, and as a link in the chain of tradition' (Ellison

R. 1964 p. 149-150.)

This mediation is the survival of some of the values, and practises used by the Griot when he operates within the context of an environment where an awareness of music, and an ability to participate is imbued with social significance. Part of that significance lies in the fact that for the modern Black performance poet, as with his archetype the Griot, poetry is an active social event, and not the solitary pursuit of the lone intellect wandering 'lonely as a cloud' as is often perceived in the Western literary tradition.

Notes on The Griot of West Africa.

1   A note on Gnaoua music: Many Jazz musicians, Randy Western in particular in his band African Rhythms incorporates Gnouan music. African Rhythms was also the name of a club that Western had in Tangier where he brought together Jazz musicians from America to perform withand alongside musicians from all over Africa, not just Morocco. His 1992 UK. tour included three Gnouan musicians from Morocco. I actually this particular line up of the band African Rhythms perform at The Northern College of Music in Manchester. I would also like to mention how Idris Shah in his book The Sufi's, defines the word Sufi as:

'to scrutinise hidden things...with the motive of concentrating the mind' (Shah I, 1968. p.180).

It is the root of the word for espionage, hence the Sufi is called the 'Spy of the Heart'. I have already mentioned how some Sufi's in West Africa are also a type of Griot who helped spread Islam throughout North Africa, and South of the Sahara from Sudan to Senegal by the use of improvised music and poetry, often extemporaneously composed to meet the moment. A book aimed directly at the contemporary diasporan Black community is Letter to An African Muslim by Shayk Abdal-Qadir as-Sufi ad-Darqawi, 1981, Diwan Press, who gives an interesting account of the role of Sufism in the political history of Africa. Other texts that deal with defining Sufis and Sufism are:

Shayk Fadhallah Haeri. 1990. The Elements of Sufism. Element Books. London, Dr.Muhammad Isa Waley.1993. Sufism The Alchemy of The Heart The Aquarian Press. London, Martin Lings. 1988. What Is Sufism Mandala. Reading. A.J. Arberry. 1979. Sufism: An Account of The Mystics of Islam. Mandala. Reading. Muhammad Abdul Haq Ansari. 1986 A.D./1406 H. Sufism and Shari'ah: A Study of Shayk Ahmed Sirindi's Effort to Reform Sufism. The Islamic Foundation. Bradford. Shah discusses the work of the various 'tariqas', pre-Colonialism, and their role in the various movements struggling towards, the respective independence of their particular countries, during colonialism.

2 The sleeve notes on recording The Pan-Islamic Tradition Vol.3 Music of Morocco Lyrichord Discs Inc. New York, LLST 7240, trace the Gnaouan tradition back to Bilal freed Ethiopian slave, companion of the Prophet Muhammad, and the first muezzin (person to call prayer).

3 G.D. Picket translator of the oral poem Sundiata: An Epic of Old Mali uses the word Mandingo to mean the people who inhabited Old Mali a vaguely defined area between the Niger and the Sankarani Rivers, not to be confused with the modern Republic of Mali (Picket. 1965. p. 85).

4 Chernoff notes how the philosophical influence of

the Griots is carried over into popular dance forms of contemporary West African music like Hi-life. He mentions how the 'sexy Highlife dancers are dancing to lyrics that say 'God never sleeps'. He continues to observe how when asking the meaning of the lyrics to a particular Highlife song, he unwittingly provoked philosophical arguments amongst his friends, who continued their debates long after he had lost interest (Chernoff J.M. 1979. p. 71). Of course this is not unusual if we consider the Sufi influence on the Griot, and Shah's notion that philosophy according to the Sufi's can be taught in many guises and there is no need to stick to one convention, thus: 'some quite happily use a religious format, while others romantic poetry, some deal in jokes, tales, legends, and others rely on art-forms and the products of artisanship' (Shah I, ibid, p.30). Its also interesting to note, in relation to the fusion of philosophy and music in Africa, and the relationship between the improvised music of the Griot and Jazz, how the origins and the meaning of the word 'Jazz', has been traced, by people like Pat Thomas, to West Africa. This is Thomas's explanation:

'The dominant religion in West Africa is Islam. the holy book of Muslims is The Qu'raan. The language of The Qu'raan is Arabic. A language used by West African Muslims is Arabic. Jazz is an Arabic word. The Hans Wehr Dictionary of Modern Written Arabic (p. 125) has revealed meanings for the word Jazz (or Jass). They are: to touch, feel, to test, probe, sound, to be a spy' (Thomas P. Rubberneck Magazine. 1993. April. p. 9). Samuel Charters in his African Journey: A Search for the Roots of the Blues, documents the styles and origins of many Griots along with translations of their lyrics. Samuel Charters. It is this lineage that inspired Thomas's essay on 'Islam's contribution of Jazz and Improvised Musics' (Thomas P. 1994. p.18).

5 Dhikr is 'remembrance', literally 'dhikr-ullah' remembrance of God. It is used to chant a particular phrase is to focus on the particular philosophical kernel within the phrase.

6 A note on 'Tartil': Khurram Murad's Way To The Qur'an, The Islamic Foundation, 1985, p. 51 describes the act of reading with 'Tartil' as ' reading without haste, distinctly, calmly, in a measured tone, with thoughtful consideration, wherein tongue, heart and limbs are in complete harmony'.

7 See John Miller Chernoff p. 36-37, 70-74, 134-140, 148-151, 153-172, 214-217.See Also St-Claire Drake who elaborates on this point concerning the inherent moral purpose, and ritualistic function within traditional African cultural activities that fused poetry and music.   The Redemption of Africa and Black Religion, 1991, Third World Press, p. 19-29.

8 See 'Bass Culture' in Dread, Beat and Blood Bogle L'Ouverture, 1975, p. 10, or hear it on the record Bass Culture Mango Records a subsidiary of Island, 1980. ILPS 9605, track 1, side 1. See also Christian Habekost, 1986, Dub Poetry ', The Sound of Drum, Bass and Voice', p. 22.
For further information on the role of the 'Bass' in Black music, see the notes on Bass frequency in Reggae International by Peter Davis and Peter Simon, Thames and Hudson, 1983, p. 54.

9 Chernoff explains the use of rhythmic complexity to instigate social awareness p. 166 & 122, the point is enhanced by the work of Kalamu Ya Salaam in his article

'It didn't jes' grew: The Social and Aesthetic Significance of African American Music', African American Review, Vol.29, num. 2, 1995.

10 Ben Sidran explains the Jazz combo, in the form of Count Basie's rhythm section, as a supreme example of 'group mutuality, of collectivity in the oral tradition'. He also explains how this rhythmic base then allowed the soloist to ride on top of the rhythm, this practise can be seen in the African drum ensemble, and also in the oral poets who ride the groove, post-Basie as it were, (Sidran B. 1971 p. 92). Chernoff uses the work of Alan Lomax from an essay called 'Song Structure and Social Social Structure' to exemplify a similar point ' African music is full of spaces. The loose structure of this musical situation gives the individual dancer, drummer, or singer the leeway to exhibit his (or her) personality in a moment of virtuosic display', Ethnology, 1, p. 448, 1962.

11 A note on the term 'Jam': it is this improvised music from Mali, as played by the Griots and Sufis, that Thomas claims to be the ancestor of Jazz as we now it today, in his essay 'Islam's Contribution to Jazz and Improvised Music', this being his main concern. Jalallodin Rumi's poetry, was extemporaneously composed, what in Arabic is called 'khawatir' or spontaneou poetry. Rumi has been the largest selling poet in America for the past 20 years. But for our purposes it is interesting to note that Thomas also, traces the term 'Jam' back to its various Arabic meanings amongst which are: gathering, collection, combination, relax, union, (Hans Wehr; p. 134-135), he cites this connection as one of the reasons why many Jazz musicians of African decent have embraced Islam. Of course Thomas's theory can also be applied to the poets to have emerged from the world of

Black Jazz. See also an album called The Jazz Singer by Eddie Jefferson it contains vocal improvisations of famous Jazz solos over the music of a Jazz quintet. Jefferson re-enacts the art of the Griot as he uses known melodies and tunes to extemporaneously compose stories on the spot. The Jazz Singer. Evidence Records ,1993. ECD2206-2

12 Lyrical virtuosity is a prerequisite not only of traditional African culture but of many of the Black oral tradition of the diaspora, Sidran offers an interesting comparison between the African approach to oral communication and the European approach, (Ibid. p.6).

The Gospel Preacher.

The performance poets from today's contemporary Black diasporan communities belong to what Ong calls 'secondary' forms of orality. This is a form of oral culture that exists on an oral-literate continuum. African American orality, especially the oral culture of the Gospel preacher is a classic example of this culture, as verified in a study by Edwards and Sienkewicz:

'The sermon of the Afro-America preacher is a specific example of such secondary orality. On the one hand the preacher is steeped in the literate culture of the book, of the Bible: on the other hand the medium of the preacher's message is purely oral.

(Edwards V. Sienkewicz T.J.1990,p. 7).

David Sutcliffe describes how the Black Church provides not only a 'spiritual anchor' but a space to develop a 'satisfying black identity'. He describes the 'world view' of the Churches as 'an oral-spiritual culture' with an aesthetic that shows a clear debt to Africa (Sutcliffe D.1986. p. 30). The first published poem by a Black diasporan was in America it was that of Jupiter Hammon, a verse of piety that appeared in a penny broadside in 1760. Evidence of the early influence of the church on Black penmanship. Rebecca Cox Jackson, Shaker eldress and Black visionary in 1836, turned to the 'Black vernacular tradition' of her foreparents after being schooled in the Bible. She did this to isolate the signifying Black difference , what Easthope describes as, 'the so-called poetry in the discourse of the other' (Easthope 1983). We can see in the space of these two brief accounts that the literate culture of the dominant society and the oral culture of the Black population both fed into what was to become the art of the Gospel preacher. We can also see the use of a linguistic divergence from the literate norm as an attempt at what Derrida describes as 'speaking' oneself free (Derrida J. 1986. p.333), to gain control over definition of the self. It is this way that the African when engaging with the medium of Christianity, used a communicative approach based on a creativity whose rules lay outside of the Eurocentric framework of reference, an approach whose rules each back as far as the thousand year old, oral traditions of ancient Mali. In order to articulate their own subjectivity, in a 'strange' tongue, early adherents to Christianity used, metaphorical allusion to subvert meaning, as in the song 'By the Rivers Of Babylon' that asks the question 'how can we sing The Lord's song in a strange land ?', comparisons to the plight of the enslaved Jews, and the enslaved Africans were functional in acquiring a new meaning for these standard hymns, a meaning that worked on behalf of Black voices. This was necessary for the very reasons that Derrida also states:

...in order to effect this translation, their common reference henceforth makes an appeal to a language that can not be found, a language at once very much older than Europe, but for that reason to be invented once more,

(Derrida. J. 1986)

To the Black slaves Christianity and the imagery and symbolism of the Bible became a language in itself when utilised by the enslaved Africans. In a rapidly modernising Europe were ideas of secular democracy and science were replacing religion, Christianity was in effect a Semitic language, in terms of discourse, and a language much older than Europe. Christianity was a language reinvented by the slaves to speak themselves free.

The sociologist Ian Miller quotes anthropologist Paul Radin when he says that:

'the ante-bellum Negro was not converted to Christianity. He converted Christianity to himself'

(Miller I. 1981. p. 6-7, p.64).

Let us examine this statement in relation to the effect of African cultural practices, on the practices of the Black Church, in particular the oral and musical aspects of ritual in Black worship. As Geneva Smitherman tells us, although the religious substance of the Black Churches has been borrowed from the Western Judaeo-Christian tradition, the process of worship has remained in practise African (Smitherman G. 1994. p. 7-9). In reference to the Griot I have mentioned, an African aesthetic that utilises rhythm, an aesthetic based on improvisation, and I would add a syncretic approach to cultural production born out of the necessity of invention. Before the contemporary Black performance poet had evolved into what we know today as the Dub poet or the Jazz poet, the potential for his existence was contained within the shamanistic role of the Black preacher, along with some of the key aesthetic practises that connected the preacher to the Griot. A prime example of this potential can be seen manifest in the life and work of Paul Robeson, singer, actor, activist, and champion of the struggling peoples of the World. Robeson's style was rooted in the Negro Spirituals of the plantation slaves, and the work songs of the chain gangs, from out of which the Gospel tradition grew, and as such was a step closer to the Root of this African orality

Sutcliffe, following on from Smitherman, outlines several speech events, found in all Black diasporan communities, that can be traced back to their roots in the Black churches. I would say further than that, as far back as their antecedents in, African forms of ritualistic communication. These oral forms have survived in other diasporan situations, where the Christian Church has been adapted by African slaves. This cultural synthesis has created Santeria in Cuba, Candomble in Brazil, Voodoo in Haiti, Hoodoo in New Orleans, and Obeah in Jamaica. Some of which remain more easily identifiable as African religious forms than others 1. Nevertheless, all possess the basic oral components, that make up the contemporary repertoires of Black popular culture. Sutcliffe lists three of the most ritualistic, as those components preserved in the speech events peculiar to the Black Gospel Churches, of the Deep South of the U.S.A., in the Mississippi Delta region. He lists them under the term 'Verbal Interaction', and they are: 'Preaching' or the 'Sermon', 'Testimony' or 'Testifying', and 'Prayer'.

To relate Sutcliffes observations to the relationship

between 2 the Griot, The Preacher and the Black Performance poet, I have collapsed them into two categories of my own, 'the Rap', 'rap' in this sense meaning merely to address a crowd with the intention of making a point 3, and 'the Call and Response' a technique aimed at gaining audience participation 4. These forms of verbal interaction fit the idea of performer and audience better, and encompass Sutcliffes 'Testifying' in the respect that both performer and audience 'testify', 'testifying,' as I see it, is as much a part of the audience response as is the improvised flourishes of the orator in full flight. These forms of 'verbal interaction' are the formulaic roots of the oral based components used by contemporary Black performance poets today. Oral formulae used to inculcate, and maintain certain values associated with the history of personal, and collective resistance, amongst diasporan Black people. One of the main acts of verbal interaction that ties the Gospel Preacher to the Performance poet, and links him back to the Griot, is the not just basic act of preaching, but the style and repertoire of oral techniques used...

'Black preachers are...verbally very flexible... and do not keep strictly to a prepared lecture. The constant in this unrehearsed improvisation is to preach in a Black style. What makes this style different is the verbal devices, and the verbal forms'

(Sutcliffe D. and Wong A. 1986.p.18-23).

In her poem ' We New World Blacks', oral poet Grace Nichols describes how :

' We New World Blacks
The timbre of our voice betrays us...
How ever far we've been

What ever tongue we speak '

(Nichols G. Hearsay: Performance Poems Plus. 1994. Audio-cassette)

Her notion of a Black voice that retains a certain identifying 'timbre' whatever language it speaks been described by Geneva Smitherman as 'tonal semantics' 5. 'Tonal semantics' is a technique that uses words and phrases chosen, and mediated, through what is mainly an African tonal system. Here is an excerpt from 'The Midnight Prayer Meeting', by Smitherman that attempts to capture in transcription, an example of tonal semantics into the written word. It is interesting to note also the use of repetition, and the strategic bursts into song by the preacher:

'I-I-I-I-I-I- love the uh-uh-uh- ha-the Lord , the Lord. He heard, he hear-d my-my-y-y-y-y-y-y cry.....AAAAA-maz-Amazing Grace uh-huh, uh, ha, how sweet, how sweet, yassuh, the sound', (Smitherman. 1977. p.138).

In addition to these verbal devices, the Black Preacher used non-verbal devices, like his cultural antecedent the Griot, and his descendant the Black performance poet, hands, feet, and the entire body at times are used to communicate. This mirrors that African norm of associating dance with narrative, and religious worship. A particular body stance may convey a particular nuance or meaning, in the heart to heart rap, as the preacher and poet alike 'tell it like it is', all means are used to tell the story, or to illustrate a point. All these devices form part of the repertoire of performance techniques, used by the practitioner of Black orality.

The second 'verbal device' used by the preacher to

induce audience collaboration is 'the call and response'. This is a crucial part of the verbal interaction in which the congregation/audience accentuate the mood and punctuate the rap/sermon with exclamations like 'Amen', 'Tell'em 'bout it', and 'Hallelujah'. According to Sutcliffe, and Smitherman, this is part and parcel of the Black oral communication, and characteristic of its African roots. In the sermon it is often prompted by things like 'Can I hear an Amen ?', or 'Can I get a witness?'.

This 'call and response' is one of the group regulating functions, a point that Chernoff in his study of values inherent within African music described thus:

'...African musical performance is so much a part of its social setting, we can recognise African critical standards by what happens in the situation itself. In such a context, everything one does becomes an act of 'criticism': people express their opinions by participating. They make a contribution to the success of the occasion, and what they do is an act of artistic participation as well'.

(Chernoff J.M. 1979. p.153).

In relation to this process as it survives in the Black Church, Dyson describes how preachers, 'refine their art in sacred settings where their verbal performances are shaped by a responsive audience that employs either ecstatic vocal support, or silent rejection on the preacher's declared truth' (Dyson,1993. ibid.p. 20). The following extract of a sermon delivered by the Reverend C.L.Franklin of the New Bethel Baptist Church in Detroit, provides an example of how, when encouraged by the audiences response, he builds skilfully on the theme of Jesus as a living force:

'Preacher: Son of man,

Congregation: Yes Lord / Yes My Lord...Oh Yeah !

Preacher: I wish you could hear him say that,
Congregation: Oh yes / Ahah go ahead (desk drumming).

Preacher: Son of man,
Congregation: All right yeah (hummed) / My Lord / Ahah.

Preacher: Can these bones Live ?
Congregation: Yes my Lord Yes! / Yes! / Yeaaah (hummed).
This type of emotive engagement with the congregation is fed by their response, and as such the role between the performer and the audience is democratised. As Smitherman remarks 'you ain't done no preaching don't nobody shout' (Smitherman. 1977. p. 151).

The audience responds in its own way, as critic or supporter of the preacher. It is in this way, in relation to the oral performer in general that successful artists shape, pace, length and content of performance by paying close attention to the expressed wishes or criticisms of those present. This spontaneous adjustment of performance leads to digressions that depend on the mood and the response of the listener. These digressions are another of the characteristics of the 'rap'. These digressions are actually a device common to Black culture in general, due its oral roots, and the immediacy of the oral experience. Improvisation, and extemporaneous composition, are characteristics of the oral African poetry forms that the slaves brought with them, forms that followed the principles of African music where 'deification of accident' was seen as the norm. This 'deification of accident', is a point of cultural aesthetics that Miler-Chernoff, notes as being linked particularly to African music, or the aesthetics of African culture. He sees this exemplified in the words of his teacher Al Haji Ibrahim Abdulai who asserts that: 'Every mistake is a new style'.

Sutcliffe describes how highly poetic language, symbolic speech, singing-talking tonal effect, group interaction as in 'call and response used to the fullest, are all part of how, in giving testimony the verbal art of a Black subjectivity is displayed. As most Black diasporans are capable of speaking a variety of 'English's' 6, ranging from Creoles, through regional dialects, to standard English, Sutcliffe cites, in reference to Caribbean church goers in the UK., how also present is the shift from Creole to standard English and back. Creole is used generally as a form of familiarity, while the use of standard English implies distance (Edwards & Sienkewicz. 1990. p.134). This is also part of the act of 'testifying', that can take place in the 'rap' or in the 'call and response', in the Church it involved also speaking in tongues and going into trances. Modern day performance poets are reinventing the act of testifying either in the 'rap' or in the 'call and response', as ritual declarations as Church expressions like 'Laawd Have mercy !', 'Praise be to God!' and 'Hallelujah' are replaced with more secular expressions like 'Keep it real !', 'What goes around comes around', or merely 'Peace !'. Having said that many Black performance poets are religious, if not Christian, and even the most secular of poets can be heard to use the expression 'Laawwd !' as a sort of symbolic link to the roots of Black orality, not just in the art of the preacher, but in a sort of traditional link between orality ritual and the metaphysical world.

The writer bell hooks has observed that:

'...the church wasn't just a place for conventional religiosity but a place for a transcendent vision of life that allowed for the formation of utopian discourses. One of the things that we ought to be asking is this. If we do away with the power of the Church, as has happened in the Black experience in the US., then what takes its place as something legitimising the imagination of a future outside of the existing social reality', (hooks b. Gilroy P. ed. 1993. p. 224)

Like a latter-day shaman it is the Black Gospel preacher who is the next step along from the Griot, in terms of the historical 'evolution' of the performance poet from Griot to the Black performance poet as he exists in the UK. today. It was the social contexts provided by the Black Churches that made this development possible. In terms of the ability of this oral performance to mobilise and politicise people within the Black community. It is no coincidence that the most significant leaders to have come from the Black diasporan community have come from a religious back ground, which allowed them the familiarity with the techniques needed for direct vocal contact with their community. This is true from the earliest abolitionist slave narratives of Frederick Douglas 7, which were performed orally at abolitionist meetings before they became written down, to the work of the Jamaican Baptist Paul Bogle, and the Jamaican preacher Marcus Mosiah Garvey, Paul Robeson, the Reverend Martin Luther King, Al Haj Malik Al Shabbazz/Malcolm X, The Reverend Jesse Jackson, and the controversial Minister Louis Farrakhan 8. All of these Black leaders are key figures in the political history of the diaspora, and all have a preaching style that fuses poetry, parable, proverb, and Black vernacular expression.

Notes on The Gospel Preacher.

1 St. Claire Drake explains the links between those religious

practises found amongst the African diaspora that are more easily recognisable as African in origin, and those which have been fused into various hybrid forms of monotheism, be it Islam or Christianity in his book The Redemption of Africa and Black Religion, Third World Press. Chicago, 1991.

2 Reverend J.M. Gates can be heard giving a sermon on Jazz Vol.1: The South selected from pre-1941 'Race Records' by Frederick Ramsay Jr. for Folkways Records FJ2801. New York 1950. For further information on the nature of the 'sermon' see: B.A. Rosenberg. 1970. The Art of the American Folk Preacher. Oxford Uni. Press, and The Formulaic Quality of Spontaneous Sermons., Journal of American Folklore 83. p. 3-20. 1970. Also 'Oral Sermons and Oral Narrative' in D.Ben Amos and K.S. Goldstein (Eds.) Folklore, Performance and Communication. The Hague. Mouton. p. 75-165. Also H. Mitchell's Black Preaching, Lippincott & Co., Philadelphia and New York, 1970.

3 At this point some sort of etymology of the word 'Rap' is necessary, in relation to the fact the term 'Rap' has undergone a transition since the emergence of Rap poetry, and is generally today understood to mean rhymed poetry spoken over a drum beat or music, this was not always the case, originally it meant 'talk' in general, like New Orleans Mardi Gras Indians 'Boss Talking'. Jazz artists like Charlie Mingus, Archie Schepp, Rhasaan Roland Kirk, Soul singers like Millie Jackson, James Brown, and Isaac Hayes, and even Funk masters like George Clinton, were all known to stop regularly during their shows and even on record, and 'talk to the people' generally in a 'down home' preaching style about some 'home truths', and some 'rights and wrongs', and this institutionalised practise was known as 'rappin' to

the people' or 'laying a little rap on the people', and it was not unlike a mini-Gospel sermon. After a short listen to the Reverend Archie Brown Lee also a Gospel recording artist, it is easy to see where James Brown got his style from, for he attended the Reverend Brown Lee's church as a youth. Many of James Brown's earlier 'raps' like 'King Heroin' and 'Public Enemy Number One', while cited on his albums as poems, are in effect evangelical discourse on the evils of drug taking in the Black community, set to music.

In the same way this evangelical didacticism is true of many Black artists today, The Last Poets echo the oratory style of Malcolm X, the style of Rap-poet Chuck D is reminiscent of Minister Louis Farrakhan, Chuck D's philosophical mentor from The Nation Of Islam. Expressions like 'I'm on a mission Ya'll', 'Can I get a witness', and 'brothers and sisters can I get an Amen', all echo the archetypal Gospel preacher's 'rap'. In the autobiographies of Dick Gregory (1965) and H. Rap Brown (1969) the word rap refers to the development of verbal strategies used as a means of coping with the harsh realities of street life. As Brown states in his autobiography Die Nigger Die !, 1969, Dial Press, New York:

I learned how to talk in the street, not from reading about Dick and Jane...The teacher would test our vocabulary every week, but we knew what vocabulary we needed. We'd exercise our minds playing the douzens... And teacher expected me to sit up in class and study poetry,...If anybody needed to study poetry, she needed to study mine. We play the douzens for recreation like white folks play scrabble. (Brown H.R. p.15).

The douzens is the name of a verbal game consisting of a competition of ritual insults, banter and repartee. The term, though not the game, is said to have originated during enslavement, 'wherein slave auctioneers sold defective 'merchandise' that is sick or older slaves, in lots of a douzen, thus a slave who was part of a douzens group was inferior' Geneva Smitherman, 1994, Black Talk, P. 100. See also , stand-op comedian, Dick Gregory 's book Nigger, Washington Square Press, 1964.

The sermon to the people the competitive douzens, and the ceremonial boasting as exemplified by Muhammad Ali, are all examples of what 'Rap' meant in its un-commodified form.

4 The Reverend Samuel Kelsey can be heard engaging in a 'call and response' with the congregation of the Temple Church of God and Christ, Washington D.C., on The Reverend Kelsey Brunswick Records OE 9256.

Johnson Lee Moore leads a secular 'call and response vocal with 12 Mississippi Penitentiary convicts on Roots of the Blues. Recorded in the field (Mississippi Delta 1959) by Alan Lomax, and edited by Lomax on London/Atlantic Records LTZK 15211. In Rappin' and Stylin Out: Communication in Urban Black America, edited by T. Kochman 1972, see A.P. Williams 'Dynamics of a Black Audience' p. 101-106, 1972, and also E.T.Sithole 'Black Folk Music' p.65-82. Uni. of Chicago Press, Illinois. 1972 Also Geneva Smitherman's talkin' & Testifying: The Language of Black America, Boston, Houghton Mifflin Co, 1977.

5 Reference to the importance of these 'Tonal Semantics' can be seen in the autobiography of Frederick Douglas, when he describes in relation to the improvised songs of the slaves how 'Meaning' was determined as much by sound as by sense. See pages 13-14 of Narrative of the Life of Frederick Douglas, An American Slave Written by

Himself.1963. Doubleday. New York..

6 Sutcliffe comments on the varieties of English spoken throughout the diaspora, by mentioning how the peoples of the African diaspora drew heavily on the colonial language whether English, French, Spanish, for their vocabulary. He describes how they had limited access to these languages in seventeenth or eighteenth century, and often only in regional forms, and what they developed was the use of European derived words pronounced in a distinctly African way, this he cites as a medium for the continuation of the oral traditions and ancestral traditions of Africa.

7 A full account of Douglas's narrative skills can be found in the introduction to the Narrative of the Life of Frederick Douglas, An American Slave Written by Himself.1963. Doubleday. New York..

8 Notes on works concerning Black leaders who have emerged from religious contexts: St.Claire Drake cites people like Prince Hall amongst some of the earliest religious leaders on record to detail the sufferings of Black people in the diaspora, in 1787. He also mentions people like Richard Allen who in 1791 was preparing the Blacks in Haiti for revolt by using religious ritual. He also adds that ' there was no group of leaders anywhere in the Caribbean during the second half of the eighteenth century equivalent to the preachers among the American Negroes' (St.Claire. ibid. p. 29). He mentions in detail the life of the slave Nat Turner the leader of the slave revolt of 1831, who after teaching himself to read and write, and after much prayer, fasting, and Bible reading, made himself a baptist preacher. Convinced that the Bible meant that all men should be free ran away in 1826.

After some deliberation he decided in 1828 to 'take up Christ's struggle for the oppressed' (Ibid. p. 39). Other texts related to the theme of Black preachers as public orators and political activists: Marcus Mosiah Garvey. Tony Martin.Ed. 1986. Marcus Garvey Message to the People: The Course of African Philosophy. The Majority Press. Dover Massachusetts.

Paul Robeson: The Artist as Revolutionary. Pluto Press.

Martin Luther King: 'I Have A Dream' (Sound/sermon) at the Lincoln Memorial, August 1963 on 'In Search Of Freedom. .Mercury Records 20119 SMCL.

Malcolm X: Bruce Perry. 1992. The Life of a Man Who Changed Black America. Station Hill New York.

Louis Farrakhan: C. Eric Lincoln. 3rd edition. 1994. The Black Muslims In America. Africa World Press Inc. New Jersey.

The Blues Men & Women.

In Chapter this section I would like to look at the secular equivalent of the Black Preacher, the Blues artist. I have taken most of my examples from a study by Alan Lomax called The Land Where Blues Began, who travelled around the Mississippi Delta during the thirties and the forties, recording on disc songs, stories, field hollers, and oral histories from the various Black people he met. Being a musician and an ethnomusicologist, he had made similar journeys, and similar recordings in his travels throughout Africa, and as such could make some interesting comparisons between what he was hearing, and learning to play in the Mississippi Delta of the thirties and fourties and what he had heard and learnt in West Africa.

In the Blues artist we also see the Griot and The

Preacher's role combined in a popular arche-type, that also eventually opened up the way for women to take a leading role in the transformational rituals of the diasporan Black peoples. People like Ma Rainey, Moms Mabley, Big Momma Thornton, Bessie Smith, and Billy Holliday are still legendary names in the Blues canon.

Samuel Charters is just one of the researchers that links the Blues artist to the Griot (Charters S. 1974. p. 2). He describes how the Griot's role in society closely paralleled that of the Blues artist. His essays are accompanied by recordings that exemplify musical and tonal similarities. The Blues artist is the Black poet writing for themselves, and the people are the imagined audience, as opposed to the 'nigger minstrel' playing for 'massah' in an atmosphere of forced gaiety. In contrast to this forced gaiety, Lomax cites how the labourers of the Deep South, floating from camp to camp, and often prison to prison, gave voice to the mood of alientaion and anomie that prevailed in the construction camps of the South:

'In creating these new, critical genres, American Blacks called upon ancient African resources, for complaints of this very type existed in the traditions of African kingdoms' (Lomax A. 1993. P. 233).

Like the Griots the early Blues artists are social satirists, 'whose verses once upon a time dethroned chieftains' (Lomax A. 1993. p. 357). Lomax describes how the Blues artists of the Mississippi Delta continued this satiric tradition depicting, as far as they dared, the ills and ironies of life in their caste ridden society. As a musicologist he adds that, most musicologists generally agree that America's Black Blues artists have, in essence, reconstituted the high art of the African Griot. As contemporary self styled Blues poet Gil Scot-Heron once said in a poetic monologue verging on a sermon:

'America gave Black folks the Blues, and Black folks just sung about it' (Scott-Heron G. 1976. Its Your World Double LP live recording).

The Griot, Preacher, and the Blues artist perform in the midst of an active and noisy crowd that 'constantly comments on and dances to their music' (Lomax A. 1993. p. 356-357). As exponents of an oral literature with a didactic purpose this something that contemporary Black performance poets have in common with the three archetypes.

Alan Lomax's excellent study of the origins of the Blues is studded with oral testimonies recorded in the field during the thirties and forties, and he has transcribed some of the humour of that period, that also characterised the Blues idiom, albeit a humour based partly if not always on self depreciation:

'Just as I was thinking
I had things all fixed up all right,
passed a tree where two doves
were making love at night.
Stopped and they looked me over
and they saw my finished plumes.
Both these birds said good and loud
'Co-oo-oooon'.

Coon, Coon, Coon,
I wish my colour would fade.
Coon, Coon, Coon,
I would be a different shade
Coon, Coon, Coon,

From morning night and noon
I wish I was a whiteman
instead of a coon.'

Lomax comments on the singer of the song thus:

'Will Stark had no problem telling the truth, but I suspect
he had forgotten how much it hurt him..."My father's
father was a whiteman" Will Stark said, "and his mother a
full-blooded Indian. all the Negro that's within me is on my
mother's side. She was a nigger".... His Black identity and
his outcast life where his mother's gifts to him'. (ibid.p.190)

Although Will Stark's lyrics seem self deprecatory
they can also be seen to be what Gates calls 'signifying' 1,
in an ironic sense, becoming a parody of himself. Houston
Baker explores the Blues as his trope for a theory of
criticism based on the Black vernacular music tradition.
Gates following in his footsteps adds the dimensions of
vernacular rhetorical devices. Gates states that:

' In the 'Blues' and in 'Signifying' are to be found the Black
traditions two greatest repositories of itself encoded in
musical and linguistic form '(Gates H.L.1988).

Mezz Mezzrow, in his autobiography Really The
Blues was one of the first commentators to recognise
that signifying as a structure of performance could apply
equally to verbal texts and musical texts. He describes a
duel between two musicians and says:

'These cutting contests are just a musical version of the
verbal duels' (Mezzrow M. 1942. p.230-378)

One particular version of this verbal duel is 'the
dozens' taken from the eighteenth century meaning of the

verb dozen meaning to stun stupefy or daze, in the Black sense through language. Today the oral poet can find himself in similar situation as Mezzrow's cutting contest in the form of the 'Sound System Clash', the 'Hip-Hop Jam', or the 'Poetry Slam', each of the above situations placing the emphasis on poetic competition of a performance nature.

What ever situation the performance takes place in the poet remains similar to what Sidran describes the first secular Black poets and musicians as being when he described them as:

'The travelling musician who has taken on the role of the truth teller from the Black preacher, the role of 'trickster' or 'bad nigger' from the devil became the ultimate symbol of freedom' (Sidran B.1981. p. 24).

Of course the symbol of the trickster otherwise known as Esu Elegba, among other names, is actually part of an old West African tradition whose origins are elaborated on in depth in Gates Signifying Monkey study. The performance poet, like the Blues artist, operating in the secular sphere is free from the traditions of the church, he/she is the preacher devoid of religious authority. In this capacity, like the Blues artist, they become the 'Trickster' whose trick lies in the mixing of the sacred and the profane, in a way that is ambiguous and characteristic of the subversive poetry of contemporary Black British performance poetry. Like the African Griot, and the Blues artist who mixes righteous indignation, with didactics and appeals to a higher authority, the Black performance poet mixes his often moralistic, and in the case of people like Curtis Watts, Jerome Masset and Muhammad Yusef, an almost religious sense of social observation, with the language of the street, and the stand-up comedy of the night club. For an example of the Blues origins of this generic hybrid, compare the following Blues lyric to the ameliorative analogy given by the Reverend Savage, in his sermon, in which assures the congregation that he can see 'Gabriel coming with the payroll on his shoulder' 2:

'Our Father which heart in Heaven
Whiteman owe me 'leven
Pay me seven.
Peace on Earth
They will be done
If I hadn't took that
I wouldn't got none.'

This is the essence of Gates's 'Signifying Monkey' trope, an impulse, or serendipity that is the 'cultural value' associated with the 'Trickster'. It is the ability to play with ambiguity, and double meaning, in an urban context that takes the Black performance poet in the UK. a step back towards his African origins. What both Sidran and Gates are referring to when they invoke the image of the Bluesman as 'bad nigger', is the spirit of rebellion, an essence of rebellion when manifest in the character of 'the trickster' or 'signifying monkey', becomes symbolic of the subversive.

The Blues artist was primarily outlawed from the 'righteous folks' of the church going community for playing the devils music in juke joints, but as a lot of preachers were deemed to be self righteous and some what corrupt in their authority, the secular testimonies of many of Lomax's witness's envied, what they termed the Bluesman's maverick, independent lifestyle. And of course by making a living travelling from town to town playing and singing, the Bluesman could make what was considered easy money at times, while partying and enjoying the attention of many women, not unlike today's rock stars. Like Robin Hood he had symbolically struck out on his own, and not only survived but prospered, albeit notoriously.

In many Blues songs, as in much contemporary Rap, which has been cited by many critics as a 'Blues' for the nineties, the anti-hero is used as a symbol of rebellion. This is expressed in Blues through the hard drinking, knife toting, womanising, gambling character of Stagger Lee, and in the genre of 'Gangsta Rap' the constant stylised use of image of the nihilistic gun toting, drug taking urban Black has merged this trope with a statement about contemporary Black inner city life that operates like a social memento-mori 3.

In the Mississippi Delta of Lomax's Blues folk, it is the 'Blue notes', those notes taken from the African pentatonic scales that formed many of the songs that the slaves had earlier brought with them. Ironically these notes are what you get if play just the black keys on a piano. These 'Blue notes' are part of the tonal semantics that add to, and form the fuller dimension of the diasporan voice. A voice denied that full recognition of its humanity. A voice of a people denied the existence of a 'soul'. This spirituality, a reaching beyond the material, is also part of what we see in the Blues, it is in Gospel, Spirituals, and ancestral African music. This seems to exemplify Gates's notion of an extreme consciousness of the metaphysical that is shared by Black people, and allows them to transcend attempts at domination in and through their complex attitudes to language and culture. It is this consciousness of the metaphysical that I associate with the role of an African spirituality as a means of cultural resistance, a spirituality, that lives on in the profane world of the Bluesman, and his female counterpart who was only later, allowed a say, due to the Church's attitude towards women singing and playing the guitar in juke-joints, and at barn dances and the like.

This eclectic, and ambiguous style of orature that uses proverbial expression, along with exaggerated image-making, yet down to earth use of metaphor and concrete references that shade into fable, and also characteristics of style that the Black British oral poet shares, with the Blues arche-type, the Griot, and the Preacher. Add to this a received wisdom rooted in a shared experience, and a common sense, that is embodied in formulaic expressions like proverbs and clichés and didactic similarities can be traced, as Miller-Chernoff illustrates, from African orature through the Caribbean and African-America 4, and I would add, right through to the poetry of many of today's Black British oral poets

Notes on The Blues Men & Women.

1 In his book Signifying Monkey: A theory of African-American Literary Criticism Henry Louis Gates Jr. ties the idea of 'double-speak' as a characteristic of Black language/ literature to the oral tradition of African-America, and he isolates the origins of what he calls a 'black rhetorical troping device' to a character from African-American folk-lore known as the 'signifying-monkey', who like his African counterpart Esu-Elegbara, tricks the Lion as king of the jungle by communicating an utterance that can be taken literally while signifying in a covert manner at the same time. This according to Gates gives a unique Black meaning to the word 'signify'. Gates.1988. Oxford Uni.Press Oxford. see p. x intro, p. 66, p. 128-129, p. 181.

2 The Reverend Savage appears in Lomax's study of how the preachers used the relative immunity of the pulpit to employ a Biblical language in their orally composed sermons that veiled their meaning. He gives the example of the Reverend Savage from Mt. Ararat Baptist Church Mississippi Delta, and describes how he uses his ability to improvise in a way that relates to the peoples lives:

'Reverend Savage began to inhale gutturally and to roar magnificently on his exhaled lines. He was dealing with the most painful part of his congregants lives-those thin pay-days when husbands brought home only a few dollars to compensate a whole family for a year of slaving in the cotton patch'.

He then adds a transcription of part of the Reverend Savages sermon:

'I see the angel coming with the payroll on his shoulder,
Servant come on home anyhow
I know you been mocked down there
I know you been crying on the way
But here come Gabriel
with one foot on the sea, and one on dray land
Pay-day gonna come, chillun Pay-day gonna come'.

Alan Lomax. 1993. The Land Where The Blues Began. p. 74.

3 John W. Roberts, in his book From Trickster to Badman: The Black Folk Hero in Slavery and Freedom, Uni. of Pennsylvania Press, Philadelphia 1990, elaborates on the relationship between the Blues singer and the Trickster in his many guises as liet motif signifying subversion. There is also an interesting note on the 'trickster' where he appears in some plantaton stories as Brer Rabbit in

the Deep South, and as Anansi the Spider in Jamaica, in A Celebration of African-American and West Indian Custom, Myth and Symbol, by Gerald Hausman and Kelvin Rodrigues, 1996, St. Martin Press, New York, p. 242.

4 In his study of aesthetics and social action in African musical idioms, John Miller Chernoff makes comparisons between the use of proverbial wisdom in Africa oral traditions and its counterpart in the diasporan communities of African-America and the Caribbean. He notes how African lyrics are especially concerned with moral and ethical questions, and how people expect their music to be made in reference to the social situation, focusing attention on, and commenting on issues of social concern. By comparing the work of Fela Kuti, and James Brown he notes how African-Americans have continued the tradition of using songs to express philosophical, ethical, or satirical themes. He asserts that this trait is so much a part of African musical idioms, that within African-American styles and songs this practise continues to serve as a guide in practical philosophy to the people who listen to it. He also illustrates how James Brown's lyrics like his African equivalent are 'thick with proverbs'. He makes a similar comparison with the words of the Calypsonians, to make the point that the aesthetic principles of African music throughout the diaspora are to an extent dependant on how the music can become socially relevant. See pp. 34, 68-74, 124-125, 164-165, in John Miller Chernoff 1979. African Rhythm and African Sensibility: Aesthetics and Social Action in African Musical Idioms, Uni.of Chicago Press. See also Worth Long's 'The Wisdom of the Blues', an interview with poet-philosopher, musician, composer and founder of Blues Heaven Foundation, often referred to as 'the poet laureate of the Blues' Willie Dixon, African-

American Review, Volume 29, number 2, 1995. Indiana State Uni.Press.

The Jazz Poets.

Jazz poetry stands as an easily recognisable bridge, a point of transition where we can see the Bluesman evolving into The Black performance poet of today. Jazz poetry is a point of confluence where the Griot, the Preacher, and the Bluesman intersect and come together. The best example of this is the work of The Last Poets, the recognised 'Godfathers' of today's 'Rap', and Black performance poetry.

The Last Poets emerged from the cultural innovations that accompanied the various upsurges of Black political and cultural activity during the sixties, as a collective of poets and musicians 1. Like many Black poets from that era they pay homage to the influence of the Blues. Last Poet Jalal Mansur Nurridin's poem 'True Blues' exemplifies clearly the way that he and his fellow poets perceived the role of The Blues in their own artistic evolution as cultural resistance in poetic form. 'True Blues' appears in print in a collection entitled Vibes From The Scribes, but is best experienced on the album 'Last Poets: Last Poets', where it is performed over an African drum beat accompanied by a haunting chant reminiscent of Paul Robeson singing a 'Negro Spiritual' (The Last Poets. Last Poets Douglas Records. 1970). In Vibes From The Scribes as an introduction to the poem on the page, Nurridin describes how the Blues represents for him ' the raw emotion emitted from the slaves as a pure outlet for their sufferings...The Lesson in the Blues is true news of a continuity of a gauntlet of soulful views'. (Nurridin J.M.

1985. p.33). The poem makes an imaginary historical link that suggests that Blues itself started back in Africa before slavery and travelled across during the middle passage, as the first lines of the poem intimate:

' True Blues ain't no new news
'bout who's been abused
for the Blues is as old as my stolen soul

I sang the Blues when the missionaries came
handing out Bibles on Jesus' name

I sang the Blues in the hull of the ship
beneath the sting of the slave master's whip

I sang the Blues when the ship anchored dock
my family being sold on the slave block...(Ibid)'.

Like many of today's contemporary Black poets the Last Poets performed their poetry accompanied by African drums, Jazz horns, and sometimes simple repetitive chants, and on three occasions I have seen them perform simply with drums, congas and bass. The conga player at the time was Abu Mustapha, a Cuban brother who played Cuban rhythms directly descended from Yoruba. Although influenced by Amiri Imamu Baraka, aka Leroi Jones, and his group of performing poets 'The Spirit House Movers', which grew from his Cultural 'Jihad' project, they became more influential on an international level. The use of their poem 'Wake Up ! Niggers!' in the controversial film 'Performance' starring Mick Jagger, projected them into a new arena with a higher profile, and more recently a cameo appearance along with Maya Angelo in the film Poetic License starring Janet Jackson as a young Black poet caught between the harsh reality of the ghetto, and her higher aspirations, reintroduced them to a next generation. The Last Poets were instrumental in inspiring Gil Scott-Heron another major figure in the interface between the Griot, Preacher, Bluesman continuum 2, and who also used Cuban conga rhythms like the Guaguanco, which he chants in the song The Bottle, asking the conga player, who he calls Doctor, to please help him, inferring that there is a Spiritual healing in the ritual use of African rhythms and ceremonial drums. The Last Poet's poem 'Die! Nigger!', is a call for rigorous revision of Black reality inspired the title of H. Rap Brown's autobiography Die Nigger Die! 1967 3.

As their career moved on their ideology moved from a form of Black Nationalism based on a Marxist-Leninist analysis of colonialism in Africa, through various forms of Maoist related ideas on cultural integrity. Their early work also shares a sort of Black-Beatnik aesthetics with people like Amiri Baraka, and travelling poet, and trumpet playerTed Joans whose seminal poem was 'Jazz is My Religion' 4. In later years some of them modified many of their earlier views and replaced them with a form of Islam based on Al Haj Malik Al Shabaz's (Malcolm X), as expounded on his return from Mecca, subsuming their racial politics and communitarian values within an Islamic framework, as did many of their contemporaries like H.Rap Brown (now Jamal Alameen), and Muhammad Ali. In the middle of one poem the drums stop and they just chant Takbir, that is:

"Allahu Akbar-Allahu-Akbar-Allahu-Akbar".

In their work Malcolm's preaching style can be clearly heard in the voice of Al Haj Sulieman Al Hadi. In the music we hear the cadences of the Bluesman, also the improvised music of the Griot in the form of Jazz played over African drums. The Afro-Cuban rhythms of the Gaugaunco and Son, as used by the then newly emergent Jazz of the times are rhythms can be heard on album tracks like 'Niggers Are Scared of Revolution' (Douglas Records 1970), and are still used by Jazz poets like Gil Scott-Heron in his track 'The Bottle' as already stated (Scott-Heron. 1982. Moving Target.).

Many UK. poet/player collectives like The Last Chant, Griot Workshop, Ras Messengers, and the Vibe Chameleons follow the example of mixing poetry with congas and brass. Groups like these also wear dashiki's and fezs , or Islamic topi's, or scull caps, which for the Last Poets is as much a part of their poetic statement as the music and the words are. This form of dress has aquired a sustained sense of ceremonial austerity amongst Black poets in Britain, and adds a sense of ritual to the performance. Musically the stylistic influence of The Last Poets is an influence that can be heard and seen in the work and performances of British Jazz poets like Jerome Masset, Muhammad Yusef, Curtis Watts aka C-Zero, all of whom perform along side congas, and Jazz horns 5. Jazz poets like Jerome Masset, Curtis Watts, and Muhammad Yusef fit very firmly into the 'Last Poets' mold, and even Dub-poets like Levi Tafari, and Benjamin Zephania, although more Reggae orientated, also bear the mark of The Last Poets in terms of certain stylistic influences, and to some extent ideological influences.

Along with Jallal Mansur Nurridin, Sulieman Al Hadi, Abu Mustapha, Gylan Kain, Omar Ben Hassan, Chuck Davis also known as Abiodun Oyewole, David Nelson formed the original 'Last Poets', who later split into two separate groups, one went more towards Black Nationalism in terms of their ideological stance, while the other followed the new international, multi-racial direction offered by Malcolm X's (Al Haj Malik Al Shabbazz) return from Mecca, and his reversion to the Sunni Muslim faith with its emphasis on racial unity. Nelson describes their first performance at Harlem's Mount Morris Park (also known as Marcus Garvey Park), at the time there were only three of them:

'I had an idea...I gave him (Abiodun Oyewole/Chuck Davis) a chant that I had heard in a video of the student take-overs at Howard Uniuversity; 'Are you ready nigger, you got to be ready. Are you ready nigger, you got to be ready'. I said 'Hey, lets take this chant, I've got a poem called 'Are You Ready', we'll go up singing this chant-the three of us-and I'll jump into my poem, and then you jump in spontaneously with something that's a response to what I'm doing, we'll just flow on through'

(Fernando S.H. jr. 1995. p.131)

Nelson also enlisted the aid of a drummer and some horn players to provide musical accompaniment, he continues:

'OK., so we go up on stage...The Musicians go up and set up, and we start chanting. Then I did my poem, and you know, they did a little ad-lib 'are you ready, are you ready', and then the next person jumped in, did their poem, then the next person, and we just did a rondo, with each of us kinda throwing in little statements completely unrehearsed...it just happened spontaneously' (ibid. 131-132).

The resonance of the Griot, and the spontaniety and group dynamics of the Preacher and his congregation, the testifying, the call and response, the musical accompaniment, are all present in the above account. Although apparently coming together, and emerging spontaneously at that moment, all these components had been there all along, in the form of the archetypal, morphic resonance's that I have spoken about. It is these archetypal resonance's that Jazz poets like The Last Poets, and their contemporaries like Baraka, Scott-Heron and Joans began using when they began to consciously politicise the Blues, and its role as a vehicle for the reinvention of a Black identity. In their attempts at the revision of the historical Black experience of creativity, and the reinscription of what Black meant, the three archetypes coalesced. I interviewed Abiodun Oyewole, and Omar Ben Hassan in Abodun's apartment in Harlem, in 1999, they had been listening to a mix of some work they'd recorded with the Wu Tang Clan, here we see the merging of Jazz poetry and Hip-Hop.

In the mini-epic poem 'Birds Word', Jallal Mansur Nurridin lists up to eighty four artists, making apologies for those that he misses out, who he claims contributed to this reinvention or reinscription of identity, that replaced the Negro, or the Nigger. The poem starts with 'everything was silent', (the enslaved diasporan Blackman had no voice). A conga starts, a double bass, then a saxophone improvising as its riding the rhythm of the drum and bass, then the poet starts the poem off by describing how:

'..and then Ma Rainey spread the Black News
by way of the Backwater Blues
as Bessie Smith picked up on it
and spread the word, thru music and song,
then the message passed on...'

(Nurridin J.M. 1985. p. 45)

By the time he ends the poem the listener has been taken on a historical journey that is peppered with references, cross-references, and a variety of intertextual signifying, in word and sound, as the saxophone player also comments and adds meaning, to the words of the poetic 'sermon', come 'testimony'.

In this poem we can hear how Nuriddin charts the development of Blues into Jazz, as a series of messianic acts of creativity that have somehow uplifted, and re-created the Blues 'nigger', into the consciously creative 'Blackman' of the Free-Jazz era, confident, and resolved enough, to hold out his hand in a guesture of peace. Nuriddin's poem 'True Blues', is a document of the historical oppression of the African, and the role of the Blues as a form of resistance in poetic form, 'Bird's Word' is concerned more with the revival, survival and evolution of a Black spirituality within the culture. It is the albums of The Last Poets, more than anyone else's, that have become seminal texts, amongst the majority of Black performance poets today. Not only are several members of The Last Poets still recording new material towards the end of the nineties, but their old stuff is being re-released in various new formats, remixed, or re-recorded with contemporary music, on C.D., tape, and vinyl records. It is a combination of their message, and the accessibility of their work that has led to this status, not to mention the need for an alternative Black voice 6.

Notes The Jazz Poets.

1 For some further historical contextualization related to The Last Poets and their work see Chris May's introduction to their book of selected poems Vibes from the Scribes, Pluto Press, 1985. Other

works worth consulting are David Toop's, The Rap Attack: African Jive to New York Hip-Hop. 1984, Pluto Press p. 116-119, and also S.H. Fernando Jr.'s The New Beats. 1984, Pluto Press, p. 129-134. Frank Kofsky's book Black Nationalism and the Revolution in Music 1970, Pathfinder, gives an interesting account of the relationship between the music of John Coltrane, and the ministry of Malcolm X, both recurring themes in the earlier works of The Last Poets.

2 'Both Gil Scott-Heron and The Last Poets are seen by most Bronx Rappers as the Godfathers of the message Rap. As a writer Scott-Heron published novels and a rap-poem 'Small Talk at 125th and Lennox' ...early Rap poems such as 'Sex Education Ghetto Style' and 'Whitey On The Moon' were in The Last Poets mold, with conga back up, other raps like 'The Revolution Will Not be Televised' used more instruments (drum, bass, flute). David Toop 1984, The Rap Attack: African Jive to New York Hip-Hop. Pluto Press .

3 See David Toop's comment on H. Rap Brown's book Die Nigger Die! in The Rap Attack: African Jive to New York Hip-Hop 1984, Pluto Press, p; 118, and also S.H.Fernando Jr. in The New Beats: Exploring the Music, Culture and Attitudes of Hip-Hop, 1995, Payback Press, p. 133.

4 A list of five recordings of Amiri Baraka performing his work, dated from 1965 to 1981 with various musical accompaniments given in Edward Kamau Brathwaite's History Of The Voice, New Beacon Books, 1984, p. 70. Ted Joans has three collections of Black-Beatnik poetry to date: Afrodisia: old and New Poems by Ted Joans, 1970, A Black Pow-Wow of Jazz Poems which is arranged into sections for reed, brass, and rhythm like a Jazz orchestra , 1971, and A Black Manifesto in Jazz Poetry and Prose, also 1971, all

published by Calder and Boyars, London.

5 The use of poetry with congas, and brass, and the wearing of fez's and topi's, with dashikis was also practised by the Jamaican collective Count Ossie and the Mystic Revelation of Rastafari. Count Ossie's line up included Count Ossie as West African termed, master drummer, a poet who was also a vocalist, and the group's double bass player, three bass drums, three funde drummers, some added percussionists, each of whom doubled up vocals along with the drummers, in terms of chanting, three horn players who between them added tenor sax, flute, clarinet, baritone sax, and trombone to the ensemble. Added to this was the voice of Bro. Samuel Clayton cited as Philosopher Orator. Bro. Clayton added sermon like narrations to the eclectic mix of Jazz and Afro-Caribbean drum riffs, poetry and song also accompanied his sermons. As a collective they have been described as performing in Jamaica what the dual roles of the Hippies and The Black Muslim's did in America by James Carnegie in the booklet that accompanies their seminal work Grounation, a three record set. Many of the poets mentioned above in connection with style of presentation, I have performed with at various times over a period of fifteen years or more, sometimes in collaborative mode for a specific arts event, sometimes in a band over a sustained period of time, as such I am familiar with their musical influences. James Carnegie another contributor to the extensive liner notes describes their performance thus: 'One does not have to be a follower of the brothers to be caught up with their presentation of history, or their poems or the hypnotic bass pluckings, or the flowing of the drums- it is like being in church when the singing is good- ANY king of church, ANYWHERE'. (James Carnegie.

1974. Grounation. Phonogram. Here we can see how all the archetypal influences have come together, the poetry, the philosophical content, the drums, the bass, and the congregational ambience of ritual healing.

6 See Kalamu Ya Salaam's 'It Didn't Jes Grew: The Social and Aesthetic Significance of African American Music' 'African American Review Volume 29, number 2, 1995, Indiana State Uni. p. 368-370. See also Bakari Kitwana The Rap on Gangsta Rap, 1994, Third World Press, p. 59, the section entitled 'Recommendations'.

7 'African and Islamic Roots of Jazz', Dr. Lloyd Miller. Utah Humanities Council.

Section Three: Live And Direct.

Freedom Flavoured Fractals

I would like to begin to look more closely at the ways in which the poetic archetypes I have spoken of have influenced UK. Black performance poetry today, with specific reference to the influence of the Jazz poetry of The Last poets. The Jazz poetry of The Last poets is the most immediate source of the archetypal influences to have impacted on Black performance poetry in Britain. It has inspired in one way or another all of the poets I have mentioned in this study, and others not yet mentioned like Jerome Masset, Curtis Watts aka C-Zero, Pauline Wiggins, Leeroy 'The Branch' Cooper, Ivan 'The Russian' Freeman, to name but a few.

As stated earlier, UK. Blacks rely a lot on the influence, adaptation and transformation of African-

American and Caribbean oral forms to construct the own forms of orature. These influences manifest themselves in the UK. as various combinations of American influenced Jazz poetry, and Jamaican influenced Dub poetry, these forms are in constant interaction with each other, and with indigenous European forms of both spoken and written poetry. Various other elements are added depending on the poets taste, or focal point of identification throughout the diaspora. The relationship between diasporan communities is complex. Similar situations to the ones that inspired the oral poets in Black communities in the US. and the Caribbean exist in Britain. Add to this the fact that many Black American servicemen stationed through out the UK. since the forties have married women from the UK., or left offspring here who identify in part with their Black American fathers, and we can see just one of the ways in which Black America meets the Caribbean in Black Britain. To illustrate how these two diasporan influences come together culturally in the form of Black performance, I will discuss the work of Muhammad Yusef as an exemplary point of confluence. His combination of styles, and his mixture of influences is very much a characteristic of the specific form of hybridity produced in Britain. Muhammad Yusef was born in London in 1959, the son of a businessman from Trinidad. He was brought up in Trinidad. At seventeen he returned to England and became a Muslim following the example of people like The Last Poets, who themselves had followed Al Haj Malik Al Shabazz, formerly Malcolm X 1. He is described in the Guardian Weekend questionnaire as 'a musical poet' whose shows 'incorporate jazz, reggae, and calypso' (Guardian Weekend. 1993. October 16. p. 78). When asked 'how would you like to die ?' his reply was 'For a cause rather than because'(ibid), this is a phrase that echoes the words of a poem by Al Haj Sulieman Al Hadi of The Last Poets entitled 'Just because your Black', the poem ends with the words :

'Niggers and Negroes
It is glorious to die
for a cause...
But not
'because'...
Just because your Black.

(Al Haj Sulieman Al Hadi. 1975. The Last Poets: Last Poets Album).

When asked which historical figure he most identifies with, he replied 'The Sufi poet. Jalal al Din Rumi' 2. It is interesting to note that Sulieman Al Hadi's co-writer and performer in The Last Poets, and apprentice, Jalal al Din Al Mansur Nurridin is named after Jalal al Din Rumi. When asked what is your most unappealing habit ?, he replies 'Collecting old jazz, blues and calypso records'. Already from this brief insight via The Guardian Weekend, we can see a stylistically hybrid path emerge that resonates with several of the strands of cultural influence that I have associated with the cultural arche-types 3. Both the Sufi poet Jalal al Din Rumi, and the Last Poets incorporate the characteristic of the Griot, many Griot's are Sufi's, both incorporate the didactic style of the preacher. Sufi's were notorious for frequenting taverns to preach to the fallen with their poetry which used metaphorical love poems to deal with issues of a spiritual nature, and some even drank alcohol, which in Islamic countries was an anathema, as such they in a way pre-dated the Blues artist as a sort of outlawed secularised preacher. Of course today's poets carry on the tradition of performing 'in taverns' as opposed to preaching to the converted, Muhammad Yusef is a contemporary example of a Sufi.

Muhammad Yusef records and performs with his band Flaming Crescent, and describes his combination of music and poetry as Islamic folk art. His album of music and poetry entitled 'The Rootical Ties of Poemology', is an interesting blend of Jazz/Blues and Calypso. Yusef as such, adds a Calypso flavour to his combination of predominantly Jazz orientated poetry. His style of delivery is influenced very much by The New York Jazz Poetry collective called The Last Poets, not only in terms of his philosophy, and visual presentation, but in his style of delivery and phrasing . His philosophy, which is a combination of Islam, via Malcolm X, and hence a certain amount of Garveyism 4, liberally spiced with Socialist allusions 5, is also very characteristic of the Last Poets . It is pro-Black without being anti-white. Certain ingredients in his music, his use of Islamic chants 6, and the dominating presence given to the congas in the mix, also echo The Last Poets. On the album cover we see Muhammad in an Islamic hat, and khaki flack-jacket wearing prayer beads around his kneck, this carries an allusion to spirituality, and a militancy that recalls the popularised image of Che Guevarra. The album cover carries the epigram:

' From the Griots of Ancient Time who were instrumental in articulating The People's Perspective. Today's artist of the Diaspora continues to use the master key 'Rootical Ties of Poemology'. Living proof that word and sound educate and entertain'. Muhammad Yusef. 1990.

The use of capitals on the words 'Griot, Ancient Time, The Peoples Perspective' and 'Diaspora', indicate his emphasis, on trying to maintain a link with a specific tradition that in some way foregrounds the interests of the collective. The use of capitals for certain words in a context when normally according to English grammar lower case would be used indicates the priorities foremost in his mind. The epigram itself attempts to outline his view of himself as a poet from a diasporan tradition, and what he sees the role of the poet to be according to that tradition. There is a sense of ceremony about his statement, a sense of ritual in his art. Although his main influences are from the genre best identified as US. Jazz poetry, the linking of the words 'word and sound' is reminiscent of Count Ossie's Caribbean Jazz orientated concept of oral poetry, and also the notion of 'Word-Sound & Power' 7, an idea often used by Rasta's to describe Dub-poetry.

From the vast panorama of Black oral poets that exist within the diaspora I have been focusing on what I have termed 'The Conscious Poets' 8. Muhammad Yusef is a 'conscious poet', when I say that I refer to the fact that there is a higher sense of purpose to what he sees himself as doing, than to merely earn a living or produce a product for the market place of popular culture. As a 'conscious poet' Muhammad is part of a group of people who transcend genre, whose unity rests in a shared commitment to issues relative to the Black community. As such it is a poetry that originates within the confines of a Black cultural experience, and is part of that emerging politicised aesthetic, spoken of by Cecil Gutzmore, which I referred to earlier.

In Muhammad Yusef's work we see the key functional components that I associate with the archetypes of the Black performance poet, the sermon-like 'Rap', and the 'call and response' above, the social commentary, and the social values inherent within those components. This 'repertoire' of functional components, that double at times as aesthetic attributes, and the way they come together in Yusef's work illustrate what Gilroy describes as 'the existence of fractal patterns of cultural and political affiliation' (ibid.p. 139). By unravelling some of the influences both stylistically and ideologically that come together in Muhammad Yusef's album 'The Rootical Ties of Poemology' we can maybe isolate some of these different cultural influences. Yusef's album contains the influence of Jazz in terms of the music, and the Jazz poetry of The Last Poets from the USA, this can be heard in 'Irangate Blues'. There is a track entitled 'LA ILAHA ILAL LAH" which is the Islamic testimony of faith, 'There is no God but The God', which asserts his Islamic beliefs, the track has an Islamic chant as its chorus adding an element of Middle-Eastern music to his cultural repertoire. 'United Queendom', a play on United Kingdom, positions him firmly as a poet living and based in Britain, as do his vocals which are a combination of Cockney tonal semantics mixed with Trinidadian nation tongue. 'Band Aid Affair', asserts a certain alliance, and identification with Africa as a Blackman, and the track 'Justice in The Streets' identifies the poet with the man in the street. The very title of the collection of poems 'Rootical Ties of Poemology', hints at how the various influences that can be clearly identified in Yusef's work are in effect 'roots' that are linked, or tied together by the form of the poetry. The oral nature of the poetry, and its musicality, all signify a cultural influence of some sort. His use of the term 'Poemology' echoes Jazz poet Gil Scot-Heron's term 'Bluesology', in its pseudo scientific mimicking of an academic term. This continual reinvention of the form, and redefining of the self is also a legacy of the cultural arche-types, and possibly the most important one, as it facilitates the adaptation and survival of the cultural values as described in Chernoff's account of the process in which:

'The continuing music consists of many rhythms, and the 'beat' emerges from the way these rhythms engage and communicate with each other. While various rhythms may be more important, no single rhythm can provide a complete focus' (Chernoff. 1979. p.157).

The poet himself, and his poetry are the only central point of unity. The performance itself is the unifying point of confluence when the musical, and linguistic tonal semantics, emerge as part of the meaning that signifies the text as part of a lived moment.

Muhammad Yusef is just one example of how, amongst Black performance poets throughout the diaspora there are many syncretic threads of influence that connect these artists cross-culturally across the globe, and synchronically across time. I have cited only a few of the examples of this form of cultural interaction, just to illustrate what I understand by the term 'fractal patterns of affiliation', and those artists, and eras as such, that have been the most influential in shaping people like Muhammad Yusef, and the many other Black performance artists that I have worked with in the past. There are no principles involved in the creative process, other than the will to self expression, within a context that links the artist to his chosen group of affiliation, whether that group be Rastas, Muslims, or Black people in general, geographically across the diaspora, historically across the generations. Each artist takes what he needs from contemporary works and also that which has gone before, to manifest in a cultural form something that speaks of and too his own experience. This stylistic borrowing liberally contributes to the overall process of hybridity that constitutes Black signification. The 'version' and the 'mix' epitomize this cross-referencing, and intertextualizing as a signifier of Black cultural production. Muhammad Yusef himself as a British born, Trinidadian flavoured Jazz poet, is a 'version' of Count Ossie, with a Last Poets 'mix'. A conscious poet like Yusef builds his culture around himself with components that give his life meaning. But in Yusef's case, as with Black performance poets in general, there is also a collective awareness at work, a consciousness that is constantly being mediated by the ritualistic submersion in the group experience.

Notes on Freedom Flavoured Fractals.

1 I have been close friends with three of the Last poets since the mid-eighties and have performed with them on several occasions, the first time being at The Everyman Theatre, Liverpool 1985, the second occasion being at The Blackie Liverpool 1986. Jalal Mansur actually lived in my street in Liverpool between 1991 and 1993. An article appeared in Black Linx published by Merseyside Community Relations Council and Liverpool Black Media Group, issue no.6, 1986, p. 5, entitled 'Last Poets Reach Liverpool'. The article was accompanied by photographs of Al haj Sulieman Al Hadi, Abu Mustapha, and Jalal Mansur Nurridin it also mentioned their collaborations with local poets, and on the opposite page appeared an article entitled The First Poets charting the emergence of local poets Levi Tafari, Leeroy 'The Branch' Cooper, Ivan 'the Russian' Freeman, and myself, it was accompanied by photographs of Tafari, Freeman and myself. Needless to say I have had many discussions with them concerning their influences and

their aesthetic principles.

2 Jalaludin Rumi's major work, generally considered to be one of the worlds greatest books, according to Rumi expert Idris Shah, is his Mathnavi-i-Maanavi (Couplets of Inner meaning). Further details concerning his work can be found in Idris Shah's The Way of The Sufi 1974, Arkana.

3 The archetypal influences that I am referring to being in this case the Griots, and the Gnaoua, who are an African-Islamic combination of the Sufi poet and the Griot. See J. Spencer Trimingham's A History of Islam in West Africa, 1970, Oxford Uni. Press. p. 80-82, 34, 109, 143-144.

4 Malcolm X's father was a strong Garveyite, and The Nation Of Islam, Malcolm's first ministerial post was led by Elija Muhammad, who was also a strong Garveyite. Hence The Nation of Islam's form of Black Nationalism was very much Garvey inspired. See 'The Autobiography of Malcolm X' by Malcolm X assisted by Alex Haley, Grove Press, 1965. Garvey was influenced by Dusé Mohamed Ali, (November 21, 1866 – June 25, 1945), was an actor, historian, journalist, editor, lecturer, traveller, publisher, and Nationalist. He was born in Alexandria, Egypt. Duse was mentor of Marcus Garvey and helped establish an organization in Detroit known as the "Universal Islamic Society." Its motto was "One God, One Aim, One Destiny." He was known to be a frequently in the company of Muhammad Pickthall, the English Muslim scholar who translated the Holy Qur'an into English. Duse Ali had considerable influence upon Garvey when they worked together in London, when Duse Ali was the Editor 'African Times and Orient Review'.

5 See 'The Black Book: The True Philosophy of Malcolm

X (El Hajj Malik El Shabazz)', edited and compiled by Yussuf Naim Kly, 1986, Clarity Press, p. 49-50 contains in a chapter entitled 'The Ideals of the People', under the subheading Socialist and Communist, an insight to what extent Malcolm X's philosophy blended the communitarian values inherent within Islam, with those of Socialism and Communism.

6 See track 3, side 1 of Muhammad Yusuf's album The Rootical Ties of Poemology, 1990, Bop Cassettes.

7 See the essay entitled 'Language And Rastafari', sub-heading 'Words, Sounds and 'Powah', by Jah Bones in David Sutcliffe and Ansel Wong's The Language of The Black Experience 1986, Basil Blackwell, p. 48-49. See also the account in Christian Habekosts book Dub Poetry in the chapter entitled 'Word, Sound, and Power', Michael Schwinn, p. 13-15. As a point of interest the term is used by Levi Tafari in his poem Dub-oetry to indicate a form of linguistic 'de-colonising of the mind' thus:

'Word Sound and Power
Come fe set we Free !
Set we Free !' (Tafari L. 1989. Liverpool Experience p. 24).

There is also an album of recorded poets in action entitled Word Sounds' Are Power: Reggae Poetry, Dub poets from Jamaica, Heartbeat, HB15, 1983, updated to CD as, CD HB15 1994. The term as used by the Rastas also bears a close resemblance to Paul Gilroy's notion of 'word and sound' as related to what he decribes as 'the problems of genre and the constant desire originally clearly evident in the auto-poesis of the slave autobiography to blend and transcend key Western categories: narrative and documentary: history and literature: ethics and politics:

word and sound', Paul Gilroy, 1995, Small Acts, Serpents Tail,p. 105.

8 When I use the term 'Conscious' I am using it in much the same way that Bakari Kitwana uses it when he beaks 'Rap-poetry' down into the three basic categories of (1) Recreational Rap, (2) Conscious Rap, and (3) Sex-Violence Rap. He adds that the term 'Conscious rap' builds upon the concept of 'Nation Conscious Rap', from the book Nation Conscious Rap by James Spady and Jospeh Eure, PC International Press, 1991. My use of the term also fits into category three and five, of the five categories set down by professor of Black Studies Maulana Ray Karenga which are as follows: (1) Player/lover, (2) gangster, (3) teacher, (4) fun lover, (5) religious.

Self Defining Black in the UK.

The diversity of forms and the cross-pollination of cultural influences that come together in the Black performance poetry of the UK., while facilitating a certain amount of creative autonomy, also serve as factors that frustrate attempts at categorisation. When asked to define his art Jazz poet Gil Scot-Heron asks , 'What do you call, Reggae, Blues, African vibration, Jazz, salsa, chants and poetry ?'. These categories are not names that in anyway allude to the possible function of these forms as seen by the artists themselves, but merely labels for commodification purposes. Designer labels realy, developed more in the interest of market forces than for their significance in relation to the social concerns of the artist.

What do you call the confluence of more than one cultural tradition, the negotiations of dominant and subordinate positions, and the subterranean strategies of transcoding and recoding, that are the mark of difference inside contemporary Black popular culture. What ever you call it to do it justice the name should in some way allude to the legacy of the poetic arche-types, the hybrid heritage of the New World African.

In relation to the long term established Black performance poets in Britain the problem of categorisation of the form is still being debated by artists and arts funding bodies. Suggested categories include 'performance poetry', 'orature', 'live art', 'time based art', 'carnival art' and an array of musically prefixed descriptions i.e. 'talking Blues', 'Duboetry', Jazz oratory', 'Jazzoetry', 'poetry on the edge of Hip-Hop'. All these titles and descriptions have been used at some point, or some time or other on funding applications, posters, and other publicity mediums, or mentioned in arts reviews, and at conferences. For example May 24-26 1996 saw the Art Black Live Two Forum, taking place at The Phoenix Arts Centre in Leicester. This is the Manchester based Black Arts Alliances second attempt to hold a conference of Black performance poets from the African/Asian diasporas to discuss, amongst other things perceptions of 'live art'. The information for the forum adds that 'Art Black Live' 'welcomes artists with a commitment to Black Live Art which draws on the traditional and contemporary aspects of our cultures'. 'Live Art' being the name chosen by the Manchester Black Arts Alliance, one of the organisations of which I am a member.to cover all hybrid forms of performance poetry. Never the less in time I imagine this definition will be revised as most of the definitions mentioned are far from absolute. Many performance poets elude a singular stylistic definition, but many jump from style to style mid poem. Many mix the sacred and the profane in a way that stops them being purely 'Spiritual' or 'Gospel', in the traditional sense, a way more like the original Griot of West Africa multi-faceted.

Despite the elusive nature of definition, two specific stylistic reference points are clearly visible as Black choices of definition; Jazz-poetry, and Dub -poetry. These two modes of stylistic signification are the most often used by performance poets as prefixes for their poetry traditionally Hip-Hop being recently added to the list of poetic genres that have evolved from the original arche-types. The choice does not always have much to do with the music that they represent in terms of mere style, these particular prefixes proliferate amongst Black performance poets because, they signify certain aspects of historical Black cultural resistance. Dub signifies an affiliation to the radical Ethiopianism of the seventies. Jazz often signifies an awareness of the anti-assimilationist unintelligibility of Be-bop in the forties, or its Islamic intellectualism and Afrocentric related Spiritual seekers like Sun ra, Pharoa Sanders, Lonnie Liston Smith's Cosmic Echoes, Steve Colman's Mystic Rhythm Society, and The John Coltrane School of Eastern Gnosis, Don Cherry's Sufi World Music. All closely visible as descendants of the four original arche-types. Many consciously aware of those arche-typical influences. All of which is encapsulated in Quincy Jones album "Back on the Block".

As discussed, ironically these 'definitions' are also part of the way Black voices have been appropriated, commodified, marginalized and trivialised by the dominant culture some of the reasons why, promoters often bill poets as Dub, or Jazz whether they are or not. This seems to point to a difference in perspective in relation to the meaning of 'style', as it is used amongst the poets, and 'style' in terms of selling point for a commodity. The difference is summed up by the cultural theorist John Jeffries, speaking in relation to Stuart Hall's notion of 'repertoires of black popular culture', he had this to say: 'for the mainstream culture and its critics, style is merely a veneer, a coating that is not particularly interesting. In stark contrast, for Black popular culture, style is the subject matter at hand' (Jeffries J. 1992. Dent G.ed. p. 158).

The Bluenote Remix Project is currently reinventing Jazz in a nineties persona that interfaces with Hip-Hop. The term Hip-hop poetry, or poetry on the edge of Hip-hop is beginning to be used by such people as the Newyorican Poetry Cafe, and The Vibe Chameleons Poetry Collective more to describe the ontological identity or their work than the eclectic nature of their poetry performances. But even as I write this the meaning of the term 'Hip-hop' is being debated in relation to its appropriation by the dominant elite as a way of Universalising, and politically sanitising what Hip-hop originally stood for when wielded as a progressive innovation by Afrika Bambaata and the Zulu Nation1 in The Bronx during the early eighties 2.

All diasporan culture is the selective appropriation, incorporation, and the re-articulation of European ideologies, cultures, and institutions along side an African heritage, Steve Coleman's Mystic Rhythm Society's, The African Way: A Multipicity of Approaches, sums this fact up. Today's Black performance poets use modern Black cultural repertoires constituted from two directions at once, the African and the European, the dominant and the subordinate. This is what makes categorisation difficult in terms of using, what have now become seen as, 'purely' musical definitions, although some types of poems do fall clearly into different categories i.e. Jazz, or Dub. Words like 'Dub', 'Jazz', are interchangeable with 'Black-conscious', on one or more of the several levels discussed, either politically, spiritually, or just in sense of Black representation. The title 'Live Art' was settled on primarily for the benefit of the regional arts funding bodies, as a title it is purely functional, and neutral in the sense that it shares none of the historical allegiances that either Dub-poetry or Jazz-poetry do 3. What it does is combine them in an apparently objective term.

At this point I would like to take a look at some of the individual, ie subjective definitions, that have been evolving from the work of the poets themselves. Definitions of that involve reference to the struggle for self definition amongst the poets themselves. Black British poet Levi Tafari following Last Poet, Jallal Mansur Nurridin's lead, coins the phrase 'Duboetry', based on a Nurridin poem called 'Jazzoetry' in which Nurridin attempts to define his art in his own words. 'Duboetry' is again the title for a poem that sets out to articulate what Tafari's definition of the poetry is in terms of form, and what that form incorporates in an ideological, and historio-cultural sense:

'Duboetry is reality
given to you inna
dhis stylee
dhis stylee come to set you free
from political captivity
dhat keeps yuh down in poverty
then controls mentally
but mentally we should be free
dhats why I chant Duboetry...'
(Tafari L. 1989. 'Duboetry' Liverpool Experience).

Here Tafari is setting down his mission statement. In a way this poem is his manifesto, his 'manifesto ars poetica' that relates the use of orality to the notion of the decolonizing of the mind. We see Tafari's awareness of the function of orality in relation to Bakhtin's notion of speaking oneself free of the meaning that comes with using someone else's language 4, he is using the language in a way that makes it his own. he does by subverting the grammar in a Caribbean manner. He is also renaming the form to make the concept of poetry his own. He is in one move defining himself, his cultural perspective, and his notion of form as being indivisible from his social reality. A function of the poem and a meaning, that can not be reproduced by just anybody reciting that poem. He is defending it from mis-appropriation in similar way to how the Be-Bop musicians did. But instead of becoming more musically sophisticated, he is making the sophistication of the Black cultural process relevant to the authenticity of the form and this way challengeing any potential commodifiers to 'Universalize' the Black. Later in the poem he acknowledges his debt to The Last Poets, and as such his affiliation to the legacy of cultural resistance

'In dhe Sixties we had Jazzoetry from dhe Last Poets
Black revolutionary
I can relate to dhat wid Duboetry...
Cos we might be living inna different country
but dhe struggle is dhe same where ever we may be...
Word Sound and Power come to set we free ! Set we free !'

(Tafari L. 1989.'Duboetry', Liverpool Experience).

Here we also see this allusion to the relationship between words, sound and power as spoke of earlier by Muhammad Yusef in the epigram to his album The Rootical Ties of Poemology mentioned in the chapter on oral polemics. 'Word, Sound and Power', being a Rasta definition in this instance of the use of orality and music as a way of liberating the mind from what he calls 'political captivity' 5. An important concept connected to the problems of trying to articulate a Black subjectivity with a white European language. Paul Gilroy defines it thus: 'the problems of genre and the constant desire originally clearly evident in the auto-poesis of the slave autobiography to blend and transcend key Western categories: narrative and documentary: history and literature: ethics and politics: word and sound' (Gilroy P. 1995. p. 105). Tafari is directly relating his concept of form to a struggle for self determination in his own community of Toxteth, Liverpool while linking that struggle to what is going on across the diaspora.

Because of the need to control the identity of the poetry, as a form evolving from an aesthetics with cultural priorities distinctly different from traditional Western literature, over a period of twenty to twenty five years or so, I have found many Black poets who have a poem in their repertoire, that sets out to define the cultural orientation of the formMany of these poems like Tafari's, if written, generally alter the traditional English spelling to attain a closer assimilation to the sound of its oral origins.

Benjamin Zephaniah illustrates this point well as he also emphasises the oral artist's association with music, in his poem 'Dhis Poetry' with a reference to the one drop rhythm of Reggae music:

'Dhis poetry is like a riddim dhat drops
deh tongue brings a riddim dhat shoots like a shot.
Dhis poctry is designed for ranting

dancehall style/ Bigmouth chanting...'

(Zephaniah B. 1990. 'Dhis Poetry', Radical Rapping).

Although Zephania is describing his poem as being inspired by a one drop 'riddim', the collection is called Radical Rapping', again showing that blurring of distinction between styles, and a certain reluctance to be constrained by stylistic taxonomy. These type of poems delineate the interelatedness of rhythm, music and poetry in terms of an identified Black aesthetic.

Black Mancunian Lemn Seisay identifies his poetry with a Black cultural perrogative associated with syncretism, music and a specifically Black orality associated with rhythm, in his poem 'Rhythms':

Rhythm ! Rhythm !
Can you hear the rhythm ?

If you listen close ears to the ground
The bass of noises rhythm sound
From spoken words to ways of walk
From rapping to reggae to funk
We talk in rhythm...

Rhythm ! Rhythm !
Can you hear the Rhythm !

In this first stanza he comments on the Black preference for bass sounds. The symbolism of 'bass', is relevant not just because it has become a distinct characteristic associated with a Black aesthetics of music, but I would suggest because it is also symbolic of the grass roots level, that is linked to the ground, being grounded, or having its feet placed firmly on the ground. Again we see the influence of the arche-types in the preference for down to earth imagery. This characteristic is often cited as one of the key aesthetic points that marks much of the poetry of the Griot, it is also mentioned in relation to the sermons of the Black Preacher, and in connection with the lyrics of the Bluesman. Seisay then uses Rhythm to link the diversity of diasporan forms, which he then relates to Black orality and movement. He then continues by linking the importance of the drum in African culture, to the suppression of cultural expression during slavery, and suggests that orality found a way around this. Again we see this allusion to the relationship between sound and power, that Gilroy mentions, and that many oral poets relate to.

'Way back in the heart of Africa they took our drums away
But rhythm proved its own power by being here today.
All four corners we'd sound with rhythm reach
We travel in a speaker even Bass in a speech...
to depth in cold heat in height
Muhammad Ali even did it in fight
With quick rhythm/ sit rhythm/ beau rhythm/ go rhythm
God given/ life giving.
Rhythm ! Rhythm !
Can you hear the rhythm ?' ( )

The crux of Seisay's poem seems to be dealing with an observation of how as Stuart Hall suggests, 'the linguistic innovations in rhetorical stylisation of the body', and the heightened expressions, ways of walking, and talking are used in Black popular culture as a means of occupying an alien space, and a means of constituting and sustaining camaraderie and community' (Hall S. Dent G. 1992.P.21-29).

Notes on Self Defining Black in the U.K..

1 See S.H.Fernando Jr.1995, The New Beats: Exploring The Music, Culture and Attitudes of Hip-Hop, p. 14-16, 46, 189, also David Toop, 1984, The Rap attack: African Jive to new York Hip-Hop., p.57-59, 133.

2 See the introduction to Fernando's study p. xxiii.

3 London based writer, performer, and cultural theorist, Michael MacMillan, ex-member of Double Edge Black Theatre Group, and currently with Raw Materials, was instrumental in the research that went into making the final decision over terminology. I did actually receive a questionnaire from him asking my opinion in regards to an adequate terminology, as did many 'Live Artists' up and down the country. His paper on the subject issued to me as part of the Black Arts Alliance's news letter, as a member of that organisation discusses the problems of terminology, and to some extent the reasons for the choice of the term 'Live Art'. See MacMillan, May 1994, Walking The Talk. 'Black Arts Practise', B.A.A. News Letter, Manchester.

4 See M. Bakhtin, 1976. '! Typography in Prose.'Readings in Russian Poetics, Formalist, Structuralist Views Ed. Ladislav Matejka & Krystyna Pomorska. Cambridge Press p. 176-196.

5 Tafari's concept of the Black mind being freed from 'political captivity' is the poets way of addressing the problem of hegemony in relation to Black peoples position as a marginalized racial group. It is similar in concept to Ngugi Wa'Thiogo's concept of de-colonising of the mind, 1986, De colonising the Mind: The Politics of Language in African Literature p. 5, 8-33. See Franz Fanon 1986, Black Skin, White Masks Pluto, introduction by Homi Bhabha.

See also Fred Lee Hord's notion of diasporan peoples of colour as colonised communities held in a sort of 'internal colonialism', 1991. Reconstructing Memory: Black Literary Criticism introduction by Houston A. Baker Jr.

It's in the Mix.

By continually reinventing, their art-form as a means of reconfigurating their identity, the Black performance poet in Britain today is recreating a source of hope, and keeping open the choice to be something other than the often nihilistic options offered by the position of Black people in British society. This is one of the elements of 'a changing same' that link the position of the poet to his original archetypes and the reality of their situation, in regards to the predicament of Black people in the historical diaspora, an historical situation that African-American cultural theorist Cornel West describes thus:

' The first African encounter with the New World was an encounter with a distinctive form of the Absurd. The initial Black struggle against degradation and evaluation in the enslaved circumstances of the New World was the struggle against, neither oppression exploitation but rather the nihilistic threat-that is , loss of hope and absence of meaning...For as long as hope remains and meaning is preserved, the possibility of overcoming oppression stays alive...without hope there can be no struggle' (West C. 1992. p. 40).

If nothing else, the overall commitment to impose meaning with a view to sustaining hope in a situation where as West decsribes '...Black folk now reside in a jungle with a cut-throat morality devoid of any faith in deliverance or hope of freedom', is what unites the above poets, synchronically to their historical archetypes. West's statement aimed at the disenchanted sections of urban Black America apply equally to their British counterparts seemingly trapped in no-win situations, from which there is little if any escape, outside of the abandonment of family, friends, neighbours, and all that is familiar. It is within this setting that the Black performance poet in the UK. comes into his own, this is the context in which he functions to the maximum of his potential as a focus of the archetypal elements. This is the context that gives the form, and the repertoire of cultural components a fuller, more significant meaning outside of the role of mere entertainment. During the live performance, the poetry becomes an act of ritual transformation, as the communal experience that it creates eludes the old image of poet as solitary thinker, not to mention the notion of poetry as the most exclusive, if not elusive of literary pursuits. In this context the poet aquires meaning in relation to what he or she isn't, without needing to define what he or she is in artistic terms. Never the less the act of defining continues to be part of the struggle to control meaning.

It is necessary to view the archetypal repertoires that embody the Black counter narratives, that oral traditionists from the Griot, to today's Black poets have struggled to voice, in the light of, what Stuart Hall has called a 'contradictory hybrid space'. It is this 'hybridity' that constitutes a diasporan aesthetic. It is this 'contradictory space', the condition of Black popular culture as a sight of contestation that can never be simplified or explained in terms of a simple binary, as in high and low, resistance versus incorporation, authentic versus inauthentic, opposition versus homogenisation, experiential versus formal, that becomes the signifier 'Black' in the term 'Black popular culture' in Stuart Hall's description of 'Good' Black popular culture (Hall S. 1992. Ed.Dent G.. p.26). As Hall asserts the factors that 'serve as the guarantees in the determination of which Black popular culture is right on, which is ours and which is not', are 'its relation to Black experience and Black expressivity' (Hall S. 1992. Ed. Dent G. p.28). As such there should be no reason why, for example a White Jazz poet shouldn't be able to create a perfectly authentic Black form in theory. From this perspective it is easy to see what David Sutcliffe means when he states that 'the term Black has primarily a cultural reference...though the racial dimension has had an effect on the culture... members of the Black community can in my view even be white' (Sutcliffe D. 1982. preface). The link between poetry and Black rituals of popular culture is important if we consider how for the African slave, ritual was the only language from which to form the dream of freedom. This dream was necessary before any form of emotional, intellectual, or physical struggle for emancipation could begin to take shape on a collective level. Like the arche-typical Griot, as custodian of a common history, this task of bringing poetry back into the network of a social and political life, is what we see being undertaken by the Black performance poet today. Like the task of the archetypal preacher the preservation, of imaginative utopian projections and much needed aspirations, are also part of that task. On another level, this is a key part of Cornel West's 'politics of conversion', and the engagement of an 'ethics' associated with love, something that relates just as much to the soul as it does to the mind, a notion that may sound antiquated to many modern ears, but as Paul Gilroy has pointed out:

'We must remember that however modern they appear to be, the artistic practises of the slaves, and their descendants are also grounded outside modernity' (Gilroy P. 1995. p. 57).

See the film; "Keeper of The Flame", on YouTube.
A film by the Punk film maker Phil Calland.

See also the novels; "The Ramblings of An Urban Dervish", & "Microwave Tea" by Eugene Lange on Amazon.

Printed in Great Britain
by Amazon

10763197R00058